The Body Book

Other Books Available in *The Lily Series*

Fiction
Here's Lily!
Lily Robbins, MD (Medical Dabbler)
Lily and the Creep—coming soon!

Nonfiction
The Beauty Book
The Body Book
The Buddy Book—coming soon!

The Body Book

Nancy Rue

Illustrated by Jennifer Zivoin

A Division of Thomas Nelson Publishers

NASHVILLE DALLAS MEXICO CITY RIO DE JANEIRO

Published in Nashville, Tennessee, by Tommy Nelson. Tommy Nelson is a registered trademark of Thomas Nelson, Inc.

Published in association with the literary agency of Alive Communications, Inc., 7680 Goddard Street, Suite 200, Colorado Springs, CO 80920. www.alivecommunications.com.

Thomas Nelson, Inc., titles may be purchased in bulk for educational, business, fund-raising, or sales promotional use. For information, please e-mail SpecialMarkets@ThomasNelson.com.

Italics in Scripture indicate the author's emphasis.

Library of Congress Cataloging-in-Publication Data

Rue, Nancy N.
  The body book / Nancy Rue.
      p. cm. -- (The lily series)
  ISBN 978-1-4003-1950-3 (pbk.)
  1. Girls--Physiology--Juvenile literature. 2. Menstruation--Juvenile literature. 3. Puberty--Juvenile literature. 4. Girls--Health and hygiene--Juvenile literature. I. Title.
  RJ145.R84 2012
  618.100835--dc23

                                        2012030005

Printed in the United States of America

12 13 14 15 16 QG 6 5 4 3 2 1

Contents

One   What's Going On in There?   6

Two   Attitude Check!   16

Three   Let's Get the Whole Period Thing Out of the Way   28

Four   When Your Period's a Pain   46

Five   Keeping Abreast   58

Six   The Whole Thing's Easier If You Take Care of Yourself: Diet   68

Seven   The Whole Thing's Easier If You Take Care of Yourself: Exercise   78

Eight   Don't Trash Your Temple   88

Nine   A Final Send-Off   102

One

What's Going On in There?

Sixty queens there may be,
and eighty concubines,
and virgins beyond number;
but my dove, my perfect one, is unique.

SONG OF SONGS 6:8-9

It's either happening already, or you've heard that it's going to.

- You're growing breasts.
- Hair is appearing in new places.
- You're sweating more.
- You've got the body odor thing going on.
- You're gaining weight or getting taller by the minute.
- Your friends are talking about starting their periods.
- You're giggling one minute and crying the next.

And in the middle of it all, you're looking in the mirror and saying, "Who are *you*, and what have you done with *me*?"

This time in your life—between about eight and about thirteen years old—is when more changes are happening in your body than have ever happened since that first year when you had to triple your weight, grow teeth, and figure out how to walk! This can be a confusing time. At certain moments you may feel like shouting to your body, "What's going *on* in there?"

Hopefully this truth will help you: "What's going on in there" is normal.

All these changes are because of something called *puberty*—and it happens to every girl, and it has since God first started making females. And probably every girl has had the same questions you might have.

GIRLZ Want to Know

❀ *LILY: Everybody talks about "When you hit puberty . . ." What is puberty anyway?*

Puberty is the time when your body starts producing two new hormones it hasn't produced before.

❀ *RENI: Great. So what's a hormone?*

A hormone is a chemical that's produced in a certain organ or gland and is then sent to another part of your body to go to work. The two new hormones in puberty are *estrogen* and *progesterone*.

❀ *ZOOEY: I have chemicals in my body?! Why? What are they doing in there?*

They're slowly turning you into a woman.

❀ *Estrogen causes*

- the development of your breasts (time for a bra?)
- the widening of your hips (think of it as curves)
- the growth of all that extra hair in your armpits and pubic area
- the production of more oil in your skin and hair (enter pimples and the greasies!)
- the thickening of the hair on your legs (break out the razor!)
- your new interest in boys (They haven't gotten any less silly. You just don't mind as much!)

❀ *Progesterone, along with estrogen, causes and controls*

- your period

How Is This a *God Thing?*

You may find yourself wanting to ask God, "How come I have to go through all these pimples and all this embarrassing hair and all this crying that comes out of nowhere? Couldn't there have been a better way?"

In *our* minds, it might seem easier to wake up one day with a mature body, clear skin, and perfect coordination—but would that really be better?

People would then expect you to *act* like a full-grown woman—and where would *that knowledge* come from?

God made growth—all kinds of growth—a gradual process that takes time. The slow appearance of hair, the day-by-day way your breasts grow, the trial and error you have to go through with your emotions—that's all part of God's plan for you to have the time to get used to the idea of becoming a woman. Hopefully, by the time you look in the mirror when you're eighteen or twenty, you're going to pretty much like what you see. The trick is to make it till then, right?

That's what this book is about: helping you understand "what's going on in there" and giving you some hints about how to grow with it, physically and spiritually.

As always, there may be some obstacles, so let's try to get those out of the way right up front.

BODY BLOCKER #1:
I'm So Far Behind Everybody Else!

Maybe you're twelve, and all your friends are getting their periods and wearing bras, but you still look and feel like a little girl.

If you have a brother who asks you, "Hey, Sis, when's the breast fairy gonna come?" or you just have the fear that you're never going to catch up, remember these things:

- It isn't a contest! You'll get there at the right time for *you*.
- You are your own unique self. God has already planned how and when you're going to grow into that.
- Meanwhile, it's who you are inside that counts anyway. If you have God-confidence, you're going to look, act, and feel good about yourself because that's just how God made you. Concentrate on God and who He wants you to be.
- Enjoy being free of bras and maxi pads while you can!

BODY BLOCKER #2:
I'm So Far Ahead of Everybody Else!

Maybe you're twelve, and you are already in a C cup and you've been having periods since you were ten. As a result, you may feel like a freak.

If you're suffering from nicknames like "Betty Big Boobs" or if people are expecting you to act like you're sixteen because you look like you are, perhaps thinking about these things will help you:

- While you're wishing you didn't have such a well-developed chest, other girls are looking at their flat ones and wishing they could be so lucky! Yet wishing won't make it so. You're going to develop on the schedule and to the degree that God has programmed in your body.

- Remember that as your age group matures, you'll get less and less teasing because other girls will catch up, and boys won't think it's so funny to give you nicknames.

- Meanwhile, if it makes you feel more comfortable, wear clothes that play down your maturing breasts and curvy hips. It's not a matter of hiding who you are; it's a way to cut down on the teasing until everybody else grows up!

- Know that God loves you and has a good plan for you, and that plan includes your womanly body. Let that give you the God-confidence to walk tall. Do not, under any circumstances, be ashamed of the way you're made. It's a God thing.

BODY BLOCKER #3:
I Just Don't Want to Grow Up

Maybe the whole idea of wearing a bra, shaving your legs, remembering to put on deodorant, and getting your period seems really scary to you.

Know that you're not alone. A lot of girls feel that way. Remembering these things may help you:

- Every girl goes through it, so share your fears with your friends. It'll bring you all closer together.

- God makes sure you have at least one adult in your life who is willing to help you figure this stuff out. Look around. Is it your mom? An older sister or other relative? A minister, counselor, nurse, or doctor? Knowing you have someone to go to who has been there (and done that!) will make you feel less afraid.
- It helps to think of puberty as sort of a path to better and better things.
- It's *fun* being a woman! We women get to have great relationships, experience incredible adventures, know never-ending love, and—someday—have babies. But to get *there*, you have to be *here* now.
- God's in it with you. He made the plan, and He doesn't expect you to follow it on your own. Prayer helps—especially when nobody else seems to understand.

Your puberty years can be fun and even a little exciting if you start by really getting acquainted with where you are now.

Who Am I?

Under each question, circle the letter that best describes you.

1. *The hair under my arms and in my pubic area between my legs*
   A. hasn't shown up yet.
   B. is starting to sprout.
   C. has been there for at least a couple of months.

2. *My breasts*
   A. What breasts?

B. are kind of raised bumps or sort of pointy little mounds.

C. have developed. The area around my nipples has gotten darker, and/or I look pretty round and full.

3. My waistline

A. is the same as it always was.

B. feels kind of thick.

C. is a real waist now. It's actually smaller than my hips!

4. My hips

A. haven't changed.

B. have ballooned out! I feel fat!

C. are finally in proportion with the rest of my body.

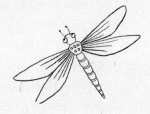

5. The hair on my legs

A. isn't that noticeable.

B. has gotten thicker and coarser.

C. needs shaving now.

6. When I take off my underwear,

A. there's nothing on them, ever.

B. there's sometimes thick, clear stuff on them or maybe something a little bit brown.

C. I sometimes discover blood. Yeah, I'm having periods.

Now let's see where you are.

If you circled mostly A's, you haven't started puberty yet—and no matter how old you are, that's okay. Puberty will happen! And when it does, because you're reading this book and asking questions and discussing your fears with an adult you trust, you'll be ready for it.

If most of your circled letters are B's, you're already *in* puberty. The hormones are working, preparing your body for womanhood. Even if you haven't started your periods, you're on your way. This waiting can be the hardest time, but it doesn't have to be. Reading this book, asking questions, and discussing your problems with a female adult you trust can make this part of your life a breeze—or at least a little less rocky.

If C was the letter you circled most, your hormones are fully operational! The worst is over; things are settling down. You're going to be very comfortable with your body before you know it. In the meantime, whatever you still may be questioning or struggling with, know that reading this book, asking questions, and discussing your problems with an adult you trust can help make the way smoother.

Talking to God About It

Let's start by praying. In the space below, write a letter to God. Pour out all the private, scary, embarrassing, I-don't-want-to stuff that you have inside. Just get it all out there. Give it to God and rest assured that He's listening. If that's hard for you, perhaps filling in the blanks in the open letter below might help.

Dear _____ *(insert your favorite name for God),*
I know this whole puberty thing is Your plan, but I have some problems with it.
For one thing, I'm embarrassed about _____.
Besides that, I'm kind of worried about _____.
And when you get right down to it, I'm just plain scared about _____.

Will You please help me not to be too embarrassed or scared to ask _____ for help?

Will You please help me get answers to my question(s) about _____?

Most of all, please help me to remember that I'm not alone and that You're there for me. I love You!

_____ (your name)

Lily Pad

My most embarrassing moment in growing up so far has been when . . .

 Two

Attitude Check!

You who are young, make the most of your youth.

ECCLESIASTES 11:9 MSG

It really doesn't matter whether you get through puberty with or without zits, with large breasts or a flat chest, with menstrual cramps or barely a twinge. No matter what, puberty's going to have its tough moments.

Maybe you'll get a pimple right on the end of your nose the night of the big dance recital. Maybe you'll start your period in the middle of a soccer game—and the coach is a man. Maybe some kid with no tact will point out to you in front of your whole youth group that you ought to start shaving your legs.

The best tool you have for getting through it all will be your own *attitude*. Let's find out what that is right now.

Who Am I?

For each statement, circle the answer that's truest for you. Be honest!

1. My body tells me
  3 when it's hungry, thirsty, tired, or sick, and I take care of it.
  2 what it needs, but I don't listen to it.
  1 My body tells me stuff? I never hear it!

2. *When it comes to keeping clean,*
  3 I'm there! I shower or bathe every day.
  2 I do it, but it's a pain.
  1 I wait until somebody makes me bathe.

3. *Exercise is*
  3 something I do a lot! It makes me feel great.
  2 something I do once in a while.

1 something I hate! Just let me be a couch potato, okay?

4. Speaking of food,

3 I eat a pretty healthy diet, even when I'm not at home.

2 I eat healthy when somebody makes me, but I'd rather have junk food.

1 I don't eat healthy. I refuse to and/or nobody insists on it.

5. When people talk about drugs, alcohol, and smoking being bad for your body,

3 I agree! I know that stuff'll hurt me.

2 I just figure I don't need to worry about it until I'm older.

1 I think they're just trying to keep me from having a good time.

6. If somebody touched me in a way I didn't want to be touched,

3 I'd tell an adult I trust.

2 I'd be too scared to tell anyone!

1 I'd figure I must have done something to make that person think he could do that.

7. Other girls I know are developing, and

3 I don't compare myself to them.

2 I know right where I am in comparison to them.

1 I think I'm a freak.

8. If I could change one thing about my body,

3 I wouldn't do it. I'm me!

2 I can definitely think of one thing I'd like to change.

1 I'd have a hard time picking out just one thing.

9. On the subject of periods,

3 I'm okay with it.

2 I'd rather not think about it.

1 Is there any way out?!

10. When it's time for bed,

3 I go because I like to get plenty of sleep.

2 I stay up until somebody makes me turn out my light.

1 I go to bed when I want, and that means I usually stay up late.

11. Emotionally speaking,

3 I have my moods, but they don't control me.

2 I feel like my feelings are on a roller coaster a lot of the time.

1 I'm in a bad mood a lot, and the people around me just have to deal with it.

12. I'm a girl and

3 I love it!

2 I mostly like it, but sometimes it's hard.

1 I wish I were a boy sometimes!

Now add up all your points.

Before we talk about your score, please know this: your number of points does *not* determine whether you are good or bad, right or wrong, a sweetheart or a real terror! Your score will help you see where you are and why you're there. It will also help you find out what you might want to work on or get help with so your journey to womanhood will be smoother and happier. Everybody wants that, right?

If you have between 36 and 30 points, you feel pretty positive about your body. You respect it enough to take care of it, protect it, and like it for what it is. Keep it up! Now look at those questions that you answered with a 1 or a 2 and pay careful attention when we talk about those subjects in the rest of this book. Don't let those areas get you down.

If you have between 29 and 20 points, you pretty much know what to do to stay healthy and to keep your body in top shape, but you aren't quite ready to do it all. Now would be a good time to look back at all the questions you answered with a 1 or a 2 and reconsider your attitude toward those topics. Can you become more positive on your own, or do you think you need to talk to someone? Read the sections in this book about those subjects extra carefully. Liking and respecting your body will make puberty—and the rest of your life—so much happier.

If you have between 19 and 12 points, you may really be feeling unhappy, and maybe that's because you haven't yet made friends with your changing body. Now is a good time to start. Find a female adult you really like and respect, and see if you can spend some time with her. Try to find things about yourself that you like and focus on those things. Read this whole book very carefully. Pray every day, as often as you can, that God will help you love and respect the body He's given you to live in. It would be sad to grow up hurting, and you don't have to.

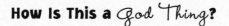

How Is This a *God Thing?*

Let's start with one of the great commandments
Jesus gave us. He said, "Love your neighbor as
yourself" (Mark 12:31). Love other people the
way you love yourself. If you don't love and
respect who God made *you* to be, you won't
know how to love and respect anybody else.
Jesus Himself said to love and take care of
your body. "But some bodies are easier to love
than others!" you might say. Only society
thinks that. God doesn't.

Pay Attention to Your Body

The second tool in making your attitude
positive—next to believing that God wants
you to and obeying Him—is to pay attention
to what your body is doing. That doesn't
mean getting so wrapped up in it that you
don't think about anything else. So what
does it mean?

GIRLZ Want to Know

 *LILY: My mother tells me to listen to my body. What
am I supposed to be hearing?*

Your body gives you signals. If you're thirsty, your body is
telling you it needs water. (Not a Coke or a chocolate shake.
Just good old water.) If you're hungry, your body wants nourishment. (Not a candy bar or a bag of chips. *Nourishment.* You
know, something healthy.) If you're tired, your body wants

rest. (Are you going to bed early enough? Are you involved in too many activities?) Do you get the idea? God made you with built-in warning signals that go off when your body needs something.

✿ *ZOOEY: If I ate every time I'm hungry, I'd be the size of the Goodyear blimp! I'm always hungry!*

Paying attention means learning when your body is telling you not only that it's hungry but also that it's full. It also means making sure you're hungry and not just bored or stressed out. We'll talk about that more in chapter 6.

✿ *SUZY: What if I can't give my body what it needs right when it tells me? Like at school. I get hungry way before lunchtime, and I always get sleepy before the last bell rings.*

Sometimes we need to adjust our bodies to the schedules we don't have any control over. Make sure you eat a good breakfast so you don't get as hungry before lunchtime. Try

getting more sleep at night and more exercise during the day to keep yourself from wanting to doze off in class. If you work with your body, it will work with you.

✿ *RENI: I don't want to turn into some kinda hypo-whatever you call it, always listening to my body to make sure there's nothing wrong with it. That's weird!*
You're talking about a *hypochondriac*, a person who lives in fear of being ill and thinks that every little ache or cough is a sign of big-time sickness. That isn't the same as paying attention to your body's real signals. When you do that, you won't stress out over every little thing because there probably won't *be* little things. You'll be healthy and happy and able to concentrate on the fun stuff in life.

Just Do It

Here are three more tools for adjusting your not-quite-positive-*yet* attitude toward your body. Try out each tool and see what helps make you happier with the skin you're in.

Try This! Look back at the quiz and choose one of the questions where you circled a 1. If you don't have a 1, choose a 2. Then, if you like to read, find a book in the library on the subject that question addresses (or go online with your parents' permission): exercise, diet, substance abuse, puberty, sleep, menstruation. If reading isn't your thing, find an expert on the subject (a personal trainer, a nutritionist, a substance abuse counselor, a doctor, or a nurse) and talk to that person. Learn all you can about the subject that is getting you down. Knowledge is great medicine for under-the-weather attitudes.

Try This! I suggested it earlier, and I'm gonna suggest it again: find a female adult you can really talk to. Your mom is probably your best choice, but if your mom isn't available or things are too strained between the two of you, this checklist may help you think of just the right person. Your person-to-confide-in should be

_____ a grown-up, at least twenty-one years old

_____ a woman

_____ a Christian—not that women who aren't Christians don't know about growing up female, but since this is a God thing for you, you'll want someone who really understands that

_____ a person you're comfortable with

_____ a person you respect: you'd like to have some of the same inside-qualities she has

_____ a person who seems very comfortable with who she is: she isn't stressed-out and nervous or always complaining about her weight or her thighs or her gray hairs

_____ a person who is available to get together with you

Have you thought of someone? If so, write her name here: _____. Give her a call. Tell her you'd like to talk about some girl issues, and ask if you can get together. Using some of your allowance to buy her a soda when you meet would be a nice touch. And of course be sure to thank her for spending time with you.

If you're still having trouble thinking of someone, consider these possibilities:

• someone at your church
• one of your teachers

- an aunt or other relative
- a school counselor or the school nurse
- a neighbor
- a friend's mom

Try This! What change in your body have you recently noticed? Are you suddenly developing breast buds? Has new hair appeared? Did you just get your period for the first time? Celebrate that change! Here are some ideas:

- Dip into your allowance, your birthday money, or your piggy bank and treat yourself to something fun.
- Invite a close friend over. Make some popcorn and pour some juice so you can "toast" your getting closer to womanhood. Celebrate your friend's most recent development too.

- Ask your mom if she and you can do something a little bit special together. Maybe you could go out and share an ice cream sundae or see a movie.
- Have your own private afternoon spa. Take a bubble bath, complete with a snack, some great music, and a scented candle (if that's okay with Mom or Dad). Enjoy the fact that you are female!

Talking to God About It

The best way to make your attitude more positive is to talk to God about it. He's an expert at boosting your thoughts about yourself. After all, He made that self just for you!

Read Psalm 5:1-3 out loud for God. If it makes you think of a psalm of your own, write it in the space below. God loves hearing from you!

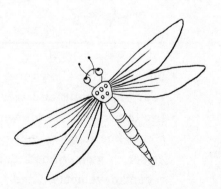

Lily Pad

The thing I like best about being female is . . .

Three

Let's Get the Whole Period Thing Out of the Way

Our sister, may you increase to thousands upon thousands.

GENESIS 24:60

By far the biggest deal about puberty is menstruation—your period—so let's go there first.

How Is This a *God Thing*?

When you have cramps or you've bled all over your favorite dry-clean-only dress or some boy teases you about the maxi pad he saw in your backpack, you may well ask, "How is *this* a God thing?"

I'm convinced God sympathizes with the discomfort and the inconvenience and the occasional embarrassment of having periods. But I also think He wants us to look at the good side of it, at what having periods *does* for us. After all, if it weren't for menstruation, we couldn't have babies. Let's look at how it works.

Reproductive System

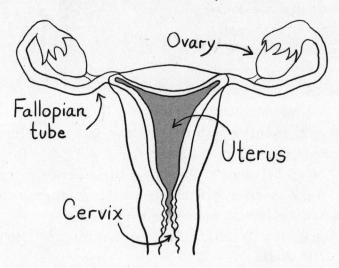

Menstruation (as the period thing is called) is evidence that your reproductive system, your baby-making equipment, is working. Inside your body are several organs that, according to God's amazing design, work together to make a baby. Check out the drawing, and then read about what each of these system parts does.

Ovaries are those almond-shaped organs that contain the eggs (or **ova**) you were born with. You started off with about four hundred thousand of them! Your ovaries make hormones—**estrogen** and **progesterone**—and once they kick in at puberty, they tell your ovaries (one ovary one month, and the other ovary the next month) to let go of a ripened egg. That event happens about two weeks before each period and is called **ovulation**. That **ovum** (singular for *ova*) then moves on to the next part of your reproductive system, the **fallopian tubes**.

See the long arm sort of thing that curves up to hold your ovary? That's a fallopian tube. It's about four inches long but only about as thick as a needle. On the outer end of each tube is a fringe called **fimbria**. The fimbria moves the egg toward the fallopian tube, and then tiny hairs inside push the egg down into the uterus so it will be in place to meet a sperm.

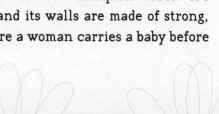

If the egg becomes fertilized by a guy's sperm—in other words, if the sperm meets the egg and breaks through the egg's outer shell—you'd be pregnant.

If the egg isn't fertilized, it moves on down the fallopian tube to the **uterus**.

The uterus—also called the **womb**—is that upside-down-pear-shaped thing between the two fallopian tubes. It's about the size of your fist, and its walls are made of strong, stretchy muscle. That's where a woman carries a baby before it's born. Right after the ovary releases the egg, estrogen causes your uterus to build a lining of tissue and blood that is just right for cradling an unborn baby. When you don't become pregnant, that lining has to be removed, so it's discharged through the **cervix** (a small opening about an inch wide in a female adult) and out through the **vagina**.

Your vagina is the passageway leading to the inside of your body. It's four or five inches long, and it can expand. That's where a baby passes through as it's born.

As usual, God came up with the perfect plan for making sure unborn babies are taken care of in the womb (the uterus) and for getting rid of whatever isn't needed all those many months when a woman *isn't* pregnant.

So try looking at menstruation this way: we women actually get to have the babies! God uses you and me in His act of creating new life! Now the whole thing just doesn't seem so bad, does it? In fact, you may even be able to see that it's a God thing!

Another word of reassurance: having as much information as you can get before your first period arrives will probably relieve most of your fears. The system God designed is totally amazing yet really pretty simple. And maybe this fact will also help you relax: girls have been having their periods for thousands of years!

How Do I Know My First Period Is on Its Way?

Here's a list of signs. See how many of these things are happening to you:

_____ You're between age nine and age eighteen.

_____ It's been about two years since your breasts started to develop and you started to get pubic hair.

_____ You've been noticing an occasional white
discharge from your vagina. That will often
happen for several months before your period
actually starts, and that discharge may even
turn slightly brown.

_____ Your stomach is looking or feeling bloated.

_____ Your breasts feel tender and swollen.

_____ You have a sudden outbreak of pimples.

_____ You feel crankier or you cry more easily than usual.

_____ You're tired and don't feel like doing much.

_____ Your lower back aches.

_____ You feel like you've gained weight, but you still
want to graze in the kitchen more than usual.

You don't have to have all of these symptoms before your period, and experiencing only one of them doesn't mean you should break out the maxi pads. But several of them happening together are a good sign that your first period could be on its way.

GIRLZ Want to Know

❀ *RENI: Okay, I gotta ask this. What is all that stuff that's going to come out of me when I get my period?*
Part of it's blood, but don't freak out. The rest is uterine lining and mucus from your cervix and vagina. (Sounds gross, I know.) It'll probably be brownish-red at the start of your period, dark red in the middle, and then brownish-red at the end. You might pass some dark red clumps called **clots**, which are just parts of the uterine lining.

❋ *ZOOEY: Am I going to lose a lot of blood? Won't I get weak?*
Not to worry. You only lose between one and six tablespoons of blood during your period. Look at a measuring spoon and you'll realize it's just not that much blood. Besides, it doesn't come out all at once. It usually dribbles out slowly over three to five days, although some girls have their periods for up to eight days, and for others, it only lasts two days. For most girls the flow is heaviest the first day or two, and then it tapers off. It isn't enough to make you weak.

❋ *KRESHA: I heard you have to douche after your period because menstrual blood is poisonous.*
First off, menstrual blood isn't any more poisonous than the saliva in your mouth or the sweat in your armpits. It's a fluid that your own body makes, so it isn't poisonous to you. What a relief, huh?

Now, let's talk about douching. You've probably seen ads for vaginal douches. Douches are liquids designed to clean the vagina, but the vagina is self-cleaning! It's like your eyes. Unless you have something stuck in your eye that needs to be flushed out, you don't wash out your eyes on a regular basis, right? You don't need to do that for your vagina either. The only time you should douche is if your doctor says you need to.

❋ *LILY: Is it all right to wash my hair during my period?*
Sure! There is no medical evidence that washing your hair during your period is harmful to you in any way. In fact, there is no *better* time to do it, because your body tends to produce more oil during your period. Go ahead and wash your hair. Looking your best will make you feel better.

❀ *SUZY: A lot of girls tell me I won't be able to swim with the team when I'm on my period. What can I do? They're counting on me. Plus, it would be so embarrassing to tell my coach. He's a guy!*

Swimming doesn't hurt you when you're on your period. It's kind of hard to disguise, though, if you aren't using a tampon. But if you use a tampon and tuck the string into your suit, no one will know you're having your period. (More on tampons later.)

❀ *RENI: Okay. One more thing. What's with all the names for your period, like "the curse" or "my friend." What am I supposed to call it?*

You left out "that time of the month" and "being on the rag" and "riding the cotton pony," not to mention "Aunt Flow." The list goes on! Personally, I think it's the names we give to our menstrual period that can make us dread it so much. It's just a natural part of what your body does. If you don't call it hate names, you probably won't hate it. So why not tell it like it is? You're on your period. It's woman time!

Get Ready!

One of the best ways to take the anxiety out of getting your first period is to be totally ready for it.

Just Do It

If you haven't already done this, ask your mom to help you pick out some supplies—preferably when your brothers aren't along on the shopping trip!—and tuck them away in a drawer next to your prettiest underwear.

Add some great-smelling sachets and maybe even a feminine treat you get to have when the day arrives. Celebrate with a tiny container of perfume, some amazing chocolate, a new pair of earrings, or a great pair of sweat socks! Make it something that will give *you* a lift.

Supplies

What kind of supplies should you get? You have a couple choices to make when it comes to feminine hygiene products (yep, that's what they're called!).

❋ Pads

Most girls start with pads because they're easy to use, and they keep things pretty simple those first few months. A pad is several layers of soft cotton made to absorb liquid. It has an adhesive strip on one side. You just peel the strip off and place that side against the crotch of your panties.

THICK

Pads come in a variety of shapes and sizes. You might try a *thick* pad (like a maxi pad) the first few days, when the flow is heavier. Also at the beginning some girls like pads with *wings* that wrap around the edges of their panties and provide added coverage. After your period slows down, you can always switch to *thinner* pads. Both thick and thin pads come with *straight* sides or with a *body-contoured* shape that some girls say are more comfortable.

Wings

THIN

BODY CONTOURED

Panty Liner

Panty liners or shields are good for that last day or two, when your period is no more than a drop here and there. You'll also find pads that are *scented*. Menstrual blood does have a slight odor, and deodorized pads contain perfumes and other chemicals to cover that. But scented pads do irritate some people's skin, so it's probably best to get the *unscented* pads and change them often to keep any smell from being noticeable.

❋ Tampons

A tampon is a narrow tube of absorbent cotton. You insert it into your vagina, and it collects the blood as it leaves your body. Your vagina is flexible, so it molds itself around the tampon, and then, because the tampon is like a sponge, it becomes larger as it absorbs the fluid. And you don't feel anything at all once you put the tampon in.

Why use a tampon instead of a pad? A tampon does have its advantages.

- Again, if a tampon is inserted right, you can't feel a thing.
- It's small enough to carry in your purse.
- There's less chance of odor than with a pad.
- You can't see it from the outside, even under a swimsuit.

So if tampons are so great, why *not* use them? There are a few reasons:

- Your vaginal opening is narrow when you're young, so you may not be ready for a tampon right away.
- They can be tricky to get in. You may want to let yourself get used to the whole idea of having periods before you try something *else* new.
- Some moms won't let their young daughters use them. If Mom says no, that's the end of it, of course. But it might be okay to remind her that using a tampon can't hurt you, it won't cause you to have cramps, and it won't make you sick. If you want to try tampons and your mother won't give her permission, go with pads for a while and bring it up again later. With a little time, she may change her mind. Meanwhile, respect her decision.

As you're gathering your supplies to put in your special drawer, you might ask some older girls what products they use. You could even get a few samples and wear them for a couple of hours before your first period ever even arrives. Just get a feel for what it's going to be like and what's comfortable for you.

✿ Emergency Kit

When you're gathering supplies, put some liners, pads, or tampons and a pair of clean undies in a small bag and tuck it into the bottom of your backpack. Why be caught unprepared, right?

✿ Dealing with It!

Even once you're prepared, you may still have some questions. And even if you're already having periods, there may be things that continue to boggle your mind.

These issues, maybe?

GIRLZ Want to Know

✿ *LILY: What's it going to feel like? Am I going to feel like I've wet my pants all the time?*
Except for possible cramps, which we'll talk about later, you probably won't feel anything more than a faint trickle now and then. To avoid that "wet pants" feeling, change your pad every two to four hours. You don't have to get up in the middle of the night to change it. Just use a fresh one right before you go to bed and another one first thing in the morning.

✿ *ZOOEY: My mother is always telling my sister not to flush pads down the toilet. But what am I supposed to do with them?*
When you change your pad, roll it into a ball, wrap toilet paper or a tissue around it, and pop it into the trash can. Public restrooms usually have a metal container in every stall for used pads. Don't flush tampons or their applicators either unless the box says they're flushable.

❀ **SUZY:** *I'm a swimmer and I do gymnastics, so my mom said I could try tampons. I'm kind of nervous. Aren't they hard to, you know, put in?*

Tampons aren't hard to use, but like anything else new, they take some practice. The first trick is to find the *type* of tampon that's right for you.

- **Cardboard applicator.** It has two tubes. One lets you insert the tampon smoothly; the other one pushes the tampon into place.

- **Plastic applicator.** It works almost the same way as the cardboard type. Some girls like it better because it's smoother.

Cardboard Applicator

- **Compact Applicator.** This works just like the plastic applicator but is compact in the packaging so it's easier to stick in your pocket or purse.

Plastic Applicator

Compact Applicator

- **No applicator.** This kind is very small and is inserted with just your finger. A lot of beginning tampon users like these.

Tampon No Applicator

After you've decided on the type of tampon, then choose the right **absorbency** and **size.** Some of your choices are junior, slender, regular, super, and extra-absorbent. Start small and work your way up. The best guideline is to use the tampon with the least absorbency possible without leaking accidents. If you're getting spots on your underwear after a half hour, try moving up from slender to regular. BTW, some tampons come in boxes with assorted absorbencies. Pretty clever!

Once you've found the tampon you think might work for you, just follow the directions on the box, or talk to your mom or another woman you trust.

That's it! Then be sure to change your tampon every few hours. If you run into problems getting the tampon in, this checklist may help:

- Are you aiming your tampon at a slant? Your vagina doesn't go straight up. It kind of angles toward the small of your back. Try inserting the tampon at a slant and see if that's easier.
- Is your vagina too dry? You could try putting a little Vaseline on the tampon. Just don't use anything with perfume in it, because the perfume can irritate your vagina.
- Are you separating the folds of skin with your fingers? If not, you may be pressing the tampon against the skin instead of into the opening of your vagina.
- Does the tampon seem too big? Try a smaller size. And if the smaller size still doesn't work or isn't comfortable, maybe your body isn't quite ready yet. It may be a few more months or even a year or two before you can comfortably use them.

In the meantime, find the most comfortable pad you can and relax. There's no need to rush conquering tampons!

❄ *LILY: I tried a tampon, but it hurt!*

That's probably because it wasn't pushed in far enough. Next time, just relax and push it in farther. If that doesn't work, pull it out and start over with a fresh one. You might also try using a tampon that expands out instead of up (there will be a diagram on the package). If you use one that gets longer as it absorbs, it may have no room to expand!

❄ *RENI: Can a tampon get lost inside me or—worse—fall out, like, in the middle of gym class?*

A tampon can't get lost inside you because the only opening from your vagina to the rest of your body is a tiny place in the center of your cervix. It's too small for a tampon to get through. And if you have a tampon in right, there's no way it can fall out. If you don't have it in right, you'll be able to feel it. If you do have it in correctly, you won't even be able to tell it's there, and it won't come out until you pull it out with the string. Your vagina is very flexible. It snuggles in around the tampon to hold it in place. There is also a ring-shaped muscle inside your vagina called the *sphincter*. Once the tampon is pushed past that, the sphincter also helps hold the tampon in place. That's why it's important to push the tampon in far enough.

❄ *RENI: Somebody told me a dentist can tell when you're having your period. How embarrassing!*

That somebody was pulling your leg. Absolutely nothing in your breath or your gums or your teeth will give you away. Besides, would it really matter if a health-care professional knew what was going on with your body? After all, what is going on is totally natural.

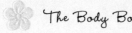

❀ KRESHA: How will I know when my period is over?

Good question! When you haven't seen any blood on your pad or tampon for several hours or maybe an entire day, you can be pretty sure your period's coming to an end. Also, the color will probably change from bright red to rusty brown. You may want to wear a panty liners for a day or two after that, just to be on the safe side. Once you've had your period for a year or two, they'll become more regular and will last for about the same number of days each time. That'll make it easier to tell when you can shed the pads for another month.

❀ RENI: So this is going to happen every month, right?

That's right. Every month until you're about fifty years old, except during the months you are pregnant, if that happens in your life. At first your periods may not be regular, but after a year or two they'll probably settle into a cycle of about twenty-eight days. That means that the time between the start of your period until the start of your next one is twenty-eight days—although for some girls it's as short as twenty-one or as long as thirty-five days. Get yourself a calendar and circle the day you start your period and the day you stop. Do that for several months, and then look for a pattern. Keeping track on the calendar is also a good way to be ready with supplies for the next one. You may even want to wear a panty liner for a day or two before you expect to start.

Talking to God About It

Make no mistake about it: getting your period is a big deal in the beginning. And although you may have an understanding mom or big sister or other female friend older than you, it's also good to take your fears, big or little, to the One who cares the *most* about you and who understands every little anxiety that you think is lame but is driving you nuts! Go to God with whatever is driving you nuts about this period thing. Want some help?

Dear God,

Someday, since I'm a girl, I'm going to get my period. And, God, here's how I feel about all that, honestly and no kidding: _____

_____.

Will You help me with that? Will You (circle all the ones you need):

- *soothe my fears?*
- *help me stop worrying?*
- *help me get prepared?*
- *help me find somebody I can talk to about it?*
- *help me see it as something exciting that's about to happen to me?*
- *make me a little gladder about being a girl?*
- _____ *(add your own if you want to)*

Thanks for loving me, God. Amen.

Lily Pad

If I could talk to my baby-making equipment in there, here's what I would say to it . . .

Four

When Your Period's a Pain

*Hear my prayer, O L*ORD*;*
   let my cry for help come to you.
Do not hide your face from me
   when I am in distress.
Turn your ear to me;
   when I call, answer me quickly.

                    PSALM 102:1-2

Even if you haven't already started your period, you've probably heard the horror stories.

"I get killer cramps!"

"I get PMS so bad my whole family hates me!"

"I started my period in science class, sitting right next to Shad Shifferdecker. What a mess! And it was all over the seat! I wanted to die right there!"

These three scenarios may be a little exaggerated, but there's some truth to each of these tales. You *can* hurt and get cranky and bleed at the worst possible times. It kind of makes you ask, "How *is* this a God thing?"

How Is This a *God Thing*?

Not everything the Bible says about menstruation is all that helpful.

Leviticus 15:19 tells us, "When a woman has her regular flow of blood, the impurity of her monthly period will last seven days, and anyone who touches her will be unclean till evening." It goes on to say anything she lies on or sits on is unclean too, and that whoever touches what she touched practically has to bathe in turpentine.

In Genesis 31:35, Rachel said to her father, "Don't be angry, my lord, that I cannot stand up in your presence; I'm having my period." And he accepted that as a perfectly logical reason for her to stay seated on her camel saddle. Yikes!

Isaiah 30:22 even compared destroying idols with throwing out a used "menstrual cloth."

Those Old Testament folks had a totally different view of menstruation than we do today. No wonder we sometimes still think of it as a curse!

But when it comes to pain and discomfort and

embarrassment, no matter what the cause, God has comfort for us in His Word. Try these on for size:

Praise be to . . . the Father of compassion and the God of all comfort, who comforts us in all our troubles.
2 CORINTHIANS 1:3-4

"Come to me, all you who are weary and burdened, and I will give you rest."
MATTHEW 11:28

He tends his flock like a shepherd: He gathers the lambs in his arms and carries them close to his heart.
ISAIAH 40:11

For I am the LORD, your God, who takes hold of your right hand and says to you, Do not fear; I will help you.
ISAIAH 41:13

These verses weren't just written for people with fatal illnesses. They're meant for all of us, no matter what kind of discomfort we might be feeling. God understands all the growing-up stuff. It helps to know that, doesn't it?

PMS, Cramps, and Other Icky Stuff!
GIRLZ Want to Know

❀ *LILY: The other day my brother accused me of having PMS and said that was why I was so grouchy. What is PMS? Do I have it?*
PMS stands for "premenstrual syndrome," and it refers to the pattern of symptoms you get before you start your period. PMS is a very real thing, caused by those hormones we've

been talking about. Estrogen is a "feel good" hormone, and its level drops before your period. When it drops, so does your good mood!

On one hand, PMS is helpful because it can alert you to the fact that your period will start in about seven to ten days. But on the other hand, PMS can be kind of a pain because it may involve any or all of these things:

- big-time hunger and thirst
- major fatigue
- feeling blue
- feeling blue one minute and *great* the next!

ZOOEY: *My mother tells me all that bleeding won't hurt, but when I hear girls talking about cramps, I get scared!*
Some girls do get mild tummy aches right before and on the first day or two of their periods. Other girls—actually very few—have pain they can't easily ignore. Nobody knows exactly why cramps happen with menstruation, but they *are* usually normal, and they're nothing to worry about. We'll talk about some good ways to get relief in the next section. For now, don't worry. Cramps very seldom keep a girl from doing the things she likes to do.

RENI: *I hear girls saying, "I must be about to start my period. I'm bloated." What does that mean?*
Bloating is a kind of swelling that happens when your body holds on to (retains) water. Usually it's in your lower abdomen, but you can also "bloat" in your breasts, hands, thighs, and even your face. No need to stress about it, though. It goes away once your period gets under way. (More on bloat relief in the next section.)

✤ *KRESHA: I started my period and had it for two months in a row, but I haven't seen it since. Do I have to go to the doctor for that?*

You're experiencing irregular periods, as a lot of girls do their first year or two of menstruating. It's a new process for your body, and it can take a while to get into a pattern. Sometimes irregular periods are caused by other things too, especially if you've been having regular periods for a while and then they get out of whack. Here are some reasons for irregular periods:

- not-so-good eating habits (you know, like fad dieting, too much junk food, and not eating enough and then stuffing yourself)
- changing your location, like moving to a new town or visiting a place with a different altitude than you're used to
- sudden and significant weight gain or loss
- big-time emotional upset or excitement
- an illness or injury
- exercise overload. A lot of female marathon runners, for example, stop having periods altogether!

How to Feel Better

But don't despair. All of the bummer things that go along with having your period can be relieved. Here's how.

Just Do It

If you've already started having periods or you're having symptoms that suggest you will soon, some of the following tips may be helpful. Read about what to do to get some comfort, and then *do* those things! There's no need to suffer. Life is not an endurance test!

❀ Cramps

- Exercise at least three times a week, even when you're not having your period. That will build up your back and tummy muscles (more on that in chapter 7).
- Stay on a good, nutritious diet all the time (more on exactly what that is in chapter 6).
- Once cramps hit, soothe them with heat. Use a heating pad, a hot water bottle, a hot bath, or one of those neat cloth bags filled with cherry pits or uncooked rice that you put in the microwave.
- If none of that helps, try an over-the-counter medication. The pharmacist can help you pick one out.
- This is pretty rare, but if your cramps are so severe they keep you in bed or totally out of things, call your doctor. He or she may prescribe a medication for you.

❀ PMS

- Again, exercise! Walk, ride a bike, swim, or play a game of tennis. Doing anything fun and active will lift your spirits.
- In addition to eating a healthy diet all the time (see chapter 6), snack on carbohydrates just before your period and for the first few days. Oatmeal cookies, pretzels, and popcorn work really well.
- Avoid too much sugar and caffeine. Go big on foods that are high in B vitamins, and that means green veggies, whole grains, and nuts.
- Get at least eight hours of sleep a night.
- Know that the grumpiness and blues you're feeling are perfectly normal, but try hard not to take them out on everybody around you. To say, "I can't help it! I have PMS!" doesn't quite make your crankiness or disrespect okay! Instead, find somebody you can talk to about it. These feelings are real, and they need to be expressed, but respectfully and to someone who will understand.
- Pamper yourself in your free time when you're "PMSing." Listen to your favorite music. Soak in a bubble bath. Take a walk with your dog. Browse through old photo albums. Reread that favorite book you've read a thousand times. Be nice to *you*.

❀ Bloating

- Get plenty of B vitamins all the time. That means be sure you're eating meat, fish, poultry, whole wheat products, leafy green veggies, and dried beans.
- Exercise regularly, even when you're not on your period (see chapter 7).

- Cut down on your salt, especially during those two weeks before your period starts.
- It sounds strange, but drink a lot of water. Water helps flush out the stuff your body is holding on to.
- If bloating makes your breasts tender, try wearing a bra that holds them firmly. A sports bra will probably do the trick.

❀ *Irregular Periods*

- Keep supplies in your purse, backpack, locker, and wherever else you spend time. You'll want to be prepared since your period can sneak up on you!
- Eat right! (Are you seeing a pattern here?)
- Exercise regularly (another pattern!), but don't overdo it (we'll talk more about that in chapter 7).
- Give your body a chance to adjust to this big change in your life. Your period will probably get more predictable in a month or two.
- Try not to let your weight change radically in short periods of time. Yo-yo dieting (where you lose a lot of weight and then gain it all back and lose a bunch more and then put it back on) is really murder on your menstrual cycle and on a lot of other parts and processes of your body as well.
- Of course, don't drink alcohol or use illegal drugs.

Do you feel stressed out a lot? Do butterflies seem to live in your tummy? Is it hard to sit still? Are you constantly worrying and maybe having some trouble sleeping or concentrating? These kinds of emotions can lead to funky cycles too. Try these remedies:

- Find a female adult to talk to about anything and everything. Start with your mom.
- Keep a journal, and write in it when things get to you. A fun journal with a cool cover and some pens in your favorite colors will make this more enjoyable. Don't worry about spelling and punctuation and all that stuff. Just spill your guts!
- Take at least thirty minutes of alone time every day and do something for you.
- Look at your schedule and ask yourself if you're doing too much. Do you really *have* to take gymnastics, ballet, *and* tap? Do they need you on the volleyball, track, *and* soccer teams all at the same time?
- Be honest with the people in your life. Don't let disagreements go unresolved or resentments build up.
- Go to God with everything. He loves you and wants to hear it all!

When Your Period Surprises You

Ask any woman if she's ever had her period sneak up on her when she had no pads or tampons within five miles, and she'll say, "Yes! Omigosh! Let me tell you about it!"

It happens to every one of us sooner or later. Know that however panicked you might feel in the moment, there's always a solution. Here are some tricks for avoiding embarrassment, collected from girls who've been there!

❀ Tricks of the Trade

Make a temporary pad out of folded toilet paper, Kleenex, or a paper towel, and tuck it into your undies. If you're at school, ask the school nurse, a teacher, or a friend if she has a tampon or pad you can use. Don't be embarrassed. Your fellow women have all been there, and they'll want to help.

If you're in a public restroom, there will probably be a coin-operated machine where you can buy tampons or pads. If you're penniless, don't be afraid to ask that nice woman who's combing her hair. Periods bond all women everywhere, and you are now a member of the club.

If blood has leaked out onto your clothes, try the old sweater-around-the waist trick. You can tie a sweater, shirt, or jacket around your waist until you can get to clean clothes and supplies. Some girls even suggest tying a sweater around your waist and then slipping out of your shorts, jeans, or skirt, rinsing it in *cold* water in the sink, and drying it with one of those hand blow-dryers you find in restrooms!

If they'll fit, keep an extra pair of jeans in your locker at school or in your backpack. Then you're always ready for a surprise arrival of your period.

A stain on your clothes will be a much bigger deal to you than to anyone else. Most people won't even notice it if you don't call their attention to it.

Think about it: how much time do *you* spend looking at other people's rear ends? If they do notice, most people aren't cruel enough to say, "Hey, Lily, you've got blood all over the back of your shorts!" Anyone who does is going to make a fool of *himself*, not you!

Just Do It

Hopefully, this business is sounding easier to you by the minute. Let's put the final comforting touch on it. Go through the following reminder checklist and mark off the things you've done to prepare yourself for the whole period thing. Then go on with the other, more fun parts of becoming a young woman.

_____ I have supplies at home, along with treats, for the big day.

_____ I have supplies at school just in case.

_____ I'm eating right, exercising regularly, and getting plenty of sleep.

_____ I'm drinking at least six eight-ounce glasses of water a day.

_____ I'm making sure I'm not doing so many things that there isn't time for me, for alone time, for the small things I enjoy.

_____ I know an adult female I can talk to about anything.

_____ I'm keeping a journal.

_____ I go to God with everything, every day.

You're set, girl! Now get ready to enjoy. Becoming a woman really can be exciting!

Lily Pad

Choose one memorable menstruation moment (it could be your own, of course) and tell about it. Ask three different females for their most memorable menstruation moments!

Five

Keeping Abreast

We have a young sister,
and her breasts are not yet grown.

SONG OF SONGS 8:8

The thing people notice first when they realize you aren't a little girl anymore is your breasts. They're the first sign that you're changing—for the better!

All Shapes and Sizes

Our breasts start to bud usually when we're between nine and twelve years old. If yours bud earlier or later, not to worry! Remember that God has each girl on her own growth schedule. In fact, nobody even knows how big your breasts will get or even how long it will take them to develop completely. We do know that they usually reach maturity around four to five years after they first begin to bud.

At first, one breast might sprout more quickly than the other, but don't worry about turning out lopsided. They'll pretty much even out sooner or later, and you won't even notice that they're not exactly alike. (They never are! Not for anyone!)

Don't bother comparing your breasts to other girls' because there are almost as many shapes, sizes, and even colors as there are women! Know your own breasts and learn to like them. They're you!

Who Am I?

Take a good look at your own breasts and then find out some interesting things about them.

1. My breasts

STAGE 1: _____ are not there yet!

STAGE 2: _____ are just little raised bumps (called breast buds). The nipples and those circles of color around them (called *areolas*) are larger and darker than they used to be.

STAGE 3: _____ are bigger than buds. In fact, they're sort of pointy, and the areolas and nipples are getting larger and darker all the time.

STAGE 4: _____ have areolas and nipples in mounds that stick out from my breasts.

STAGE 5: _____ have a full, round shape, and the nipples are kind of raised. It's been about four years since I just had little buds.

Remember that each stage is a normal step in the development of your breasts. It can be kinda fun to notice them growing and changing. If you have a little tenderness with each stage, don't worry. These are just growing pains.

2. My breasts are/have (circle the word/phrase in each pair that best describes you at the moment):

round	pointy
high on my chest	low on my chest
pointed up	pointed down
pink in the areola	brown in the areola
nipples that go outward	nipples that go inward
hairs around the areola	hairless

Looking at your own combination, think how many different combos are possible. God planned them all. Every breast is a beautiful thing that may someday be used to nurse a precious baby. Your breasts are a lovely part of your womanhood. Enjoy!

Bras

Once your breast buds start to appear, you'll probably think about the bra issue. How do you know when, what kind, and what size?

GIRLZ Want to Know

❁ *SUZY: I think I need a bra, but I'm not sure. How do I know?*

The best rule of thumb is your answer to this question: Are you more comfortable with a bra than without one? You also might ask yourself these questions:

- Do I feel funky because my new breasts show through my clothes?
- Do I get self-conscious because I notice my breasts jiggling when I'm active?
- Do my breasts hurt when I play sports?

If you answered yes to at least one of these questions, you're probably ready for a bra.

❁ *RENI: I answered no to all those questions, but all my friends have bras, and I feel like a geek. A baby geek.*

There's nothing wrong with wearing an A, AA, or AAA cup bra (more on that later) even if you don't "need" one. Or you can wear a pretty camisole to make you feel feminine and grown-up. Tank tops and sports bras are great for that too. It's no fun feeling left out, and in this case, it's so easy to fix.

❁ *ZOOEY: I know I need a bra, but my mom doesn't really want me to grow up. How do I ask her without her getting all freaked out?*

Most moms are pretty impressed when their daughters surprise them with their maturity. Think about why you want a bra. Then, when your mom isn't distracted and you two are alone, go to her and state your case calmly and politely. (I'd suggest leaving out "Everybody else has one!") Ask her if she'll go shopping with you and help you pick one out. I would really advise against going shopping with your friends or buying your first one on your own. Moms really like to be included in those important events. And I know you know this: it's never okay to go behind a parent's back.

If your mom says no, try putting a snug tank top under your shirt to help keep your breasts in place and keep you from feeling self-conscious until she changes her mind. She will—especially when she sees how maturely you're reacting to her saying, "Not yet."

❀ *LILY: I wear a bra already, and my brothers tease me about it constantly. I know the boys at school are making comments behind my back, mostly because I'm one of the first girls in our class to have one. I really hate feeling like they're all talking about my bra.*

There's not much you can do about what they say. Some people just become socially mature faster than others. Until those boys do grow up and get a life, you may want to get your mom to buy you some bras in neutral colors that blend in with your skin. You might get them in a plain, smooth style without lace and bows. It isn't that you're trying to hide something. You're just avoiding the boys giving you a hard time. It's okay to make life easier on yourself.

❀ *KRESHA: How do I know what size to get? I just don't understand all those letters and numbers!*

Bra sizes have two parts: a number for the size of your rib cage and a letter for the size of your breast, called a cup size. You'll see combinations like 32A, 34B, 36A, and so on.

❀ *Here's how you figure out your size:*

1. Measure around your ribs just below your breasts.
2. Find your rib measurement on the right.

22-23 inches	➞	**28**
24-25 inches	➞	**30**
26-27 inches	➞	**32**
28-29 inches	➞	**34**
30-31 inches	➞	**36**

3. Now measure around your chest, right over your nipples.
4. Subtract your rib number (step 2) from your chest number (step 3).
5. Look for the number you get on the left below and you will find your cup size on the right.

-1	**AAA**
0	**AA**
1	**A**
2	**B**
3	**C**
4	**D**

6. Your bra size is your rib number and your cup size together. Write it here: _____ But don't expect every bra labeled with your size to fit perfectly. Different

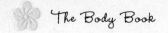

styles will fit differently, so just use your bra size as a place to start looking. You'll know a bra fits when it

- looks smooth under your shirt;
- doesn't pinch you anywhere;
- doesn't ride up in the back; and
- doesn't slide off your shoulders.

Don't forget that you can adjust the size of a bra a little bit by moving the hook over one or two notches. Most bras also have adjustable straps so you can make them snug but comfortable.

❀ *LILY: There are so many different styles! I get totally confused. How do I know where to start?*
Just like everything else you can buy, bras come in a variety of styles, fabrics, and colors. Fabrics and colors are just a matter of taste. Styles come in several different types. Here are four:

- "Training" bras don't actually train your breasts! A training bra just helps you get comfortable with wearing a bra. Trainers come in A, AA, and AAA.
- Soft cup bras are soft and flexible with an elastic band just under your breasts. This provides enough support for most girls who wear a B cup or smaller. A soft cup bra is definitely comfortable when it fits right.
- Underwire bras have a curved wire sewn in under each cup to give girls in C cup or higher the support they need to cut down on jiggling. An underwire bra is a little bit stiff, but it can still be comfy.
- Sports bras are made for wearing—you guessed it!— while you're playing sports, running, and generally being active. A sports bra is basically a tank top that comes just below your breasts and fits snug so your

breasts stay in place and are pain-free when you're on the go. Some girls feel so comfortable in sports bras that they wear them all the time.

❀ *ZOOEY: When I do finally get a bra, I'm going to want to wear it day and night! Is that okay?*
Actually, there's really no reason to wear a bra to bed. It's nice to get a break while you sleep.

Too Big! Too Small!

For some reason, a lot of American girls think they have to have the perfect breasts, with *perfect* meaning "round, full, and spilling out of their blouses" or "small, perky, and hiding daintily under their tank tops." Hopefully, you've figured out by now that the perfect breasts for you are the ones you have.

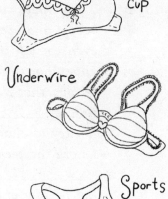

Training

Soft Cup

Underwire

Sports

It's tough, though, when girls with a build that's a lot like yours express their discontentment. It can be contagious! Have you heard these complaints or maybe even had them yourself?

"I'm so flat-chested, and everybody teases me about it. I feel like a boy!"

"If the breast fairy doesn't come soon, I'm going to save up and buy one of those increase-your-bust things I see in the back of magazines."

"I get so sick of having nothing up top. I stuff Kleenex, washcloths, anything I can find in my training bra so at least I look normal!"

65

"I have the biggest breasts on the planet for a girl my age. Nobody in my class wears a C cup. The boys call me Dolly Parton, and I hate that!"

"I'm embarrassed to take my bra off in front of my friends in PE or at sleepovers because I have these weird hairs around my nipples. That hair makes me feel like I'm part male!"

Even if adults or your girlfriends don't think your problem is such a big deal, it can be painful for you. That's when the best One to go to is God.

Talking to God About It

As always, it's good to just go to your quiet place and pour out to God all your feelings. You can talk out loud, write in your journal, or keep your thoughts in your head. Any option can be helpful! If you need a nudge to get started, here's a God-conversation starter.

Dear _____ *(your favorite way of addressing God),*

I'm having some problems with this breast thing. I know I'm supposed to like my body just the way You made it, but I need Your help with that. Would You please help me:
- *accept and appreciate these breasts You've given me, even though they're* _____
- *know that it isn't just my breasts that make me female, that I am a girl through and through in spite of* _____
- *not try to change my breasts by* _____
- *ignore the teasing and pray for the teasers, like* ____
  _____
- *not let any of this upset me so much that I miss out on the fun of becoming a young woman.*
  Amen,
  _____*(your name)*

Remember that God loves you, that He has good plans for you, that He knows what you're going through to get there, and that He's with you every step of the way. All of those facts have gotta help.

Lily Pad

The perfect bra for me would look and feel like . . .

Six

The Whole Thing's Easier If You Take Care of Yourself:

Diet

God said, "I give you every seed-bearing plant on the face of the whole earth and every tree that has fruit with seed in it. They will be yours for food."

GENESIS 1:29

Could anything be more boring than reading about what foods you should eat?

Well, yeah. We could discuss the exports of Peru, or prime numbers, or today's interest rates . . .

There *are* less interesting topics than food, and nutrition really *can* be fun to think about. And did you realize that the one thing that, more than anything else, influences the way you look and feel is . . . drum-roll! . . . your diet?

Besides, God says we need to think about what we eat.

How Is This a *God Thing*?

In the Bible, there are literally *hundreds* of references to food, everything from what to eat—milk, butter, cheese, bread, corn, fish, flesh (relax! it means meat!), herbs, fruit, honey, oil, and vinegar—to how to prepare it. From what *not* to eat—badger and camel (like we *would*!)—to how much to eat. From whom to eat with to where to sit at the table.

But Paul summed it up the best for us in Romans 14:17 when he said, "For the kingdom of God is not a matter of eating and drinking, but of righteousness, peace and joy in the Holy Spirit."

Food, he went on to say in 1 Corinthians 8:8, doesn't bring us nearer to God. But the way we take care of our bodies *does* help us have a better relationship with God. Paul also wrote this: "God's temple is sacred, and you are that temple" (1 Corinthians 3:17). You have to feed that body of yours right, or you aren't taking care of your temple.

Delicate Balance

You're growing right now, so it's more important than ever to give yourself a wide variety of foods. The trick is to eat enough of the most nutritious foods (the veggies and fruits and whole grains) and not too much of the stuff that's high in fat and sugar (the Snickers bars and the potato chips). Sounds pretty simple, doesn't it?

Who Am I?

Before we start this quiz, you need to make sure you know what a *serving* is, since the questions ask you how many servings of something you eat every day. The serving size is different for different foods, but this list of examples might give you a general idea:

- Bread—1 slice
- Cereal—1/2 cup
- Veggies—a pile about the size of your fist
- Apple—1 medium-sized
- Strawberries—1 cup
- Milk—1 cup
- Cheese—1 hunk, golf-ball size
- Hamburger—1 patty about the size of a deck of cards
- M&M's—one small handful

Read each question that follows. Then circle the number of servings you eat on an average day. (Be honest, of course!) You may have to pay attention to what you eat for a day or two before you can answer some of these questions. One more thing: of course no one eats exactly the same thing every day, but try to think about what you put away during a typical twenty-four-hour period.

1. *How many servings of bread, cereal, tortillas, rice, pasta, or any other kind of grain-thing do you eat every day?*

   10 9 8 7 6 5 4 3 2 1 0

2. *How many servings of veggies do you eat every day?*

   10 9 8 7 6 5 4 3 2 1 0

3. *How many servings of fruit do you eat every day, including fruit juice with no added sugar?*

   10 9 8 7 6 5 4 3 2 1 0

4. *How many servings of dairy products, like milk, cheese, cottage cheese, and yogurt, do you eat every day?*

   10 9 8 7 6 5 4 3 2 1 0

5. *How many servings of meat, including chicken and fish, do you eat every day?*

   10 9 8 7 6 5 4 3 2 1 0

6. *How many servings of fats, oils, and sweets (things like candy, sodas, salad dressings, and assorted junk food) do you eat each day?*

   10 9 8 7 6 5 4 3 2 1 0

Now take a look at the ChooseMyPlate diagram and see how your eating habits fit. (This plate, by the way, is recommended by some folks who devote their lives to helping people eat well.) Every time you sit down for a meal, be sure you have something from all the food groups—fruits, vegetables, grain, protein, and dairy. Did you notice that half your plate is supposed to be covered by fruits and vegetables? The experts also suggest that you get protein from different sources, that you switch to 2 percent or 1 percent milk, and that half the grains you eat are whole grains. And go easy on sugar, salt, and fat. (For more details and even a personal food plan, go to ChooseMyPlate.gov.)

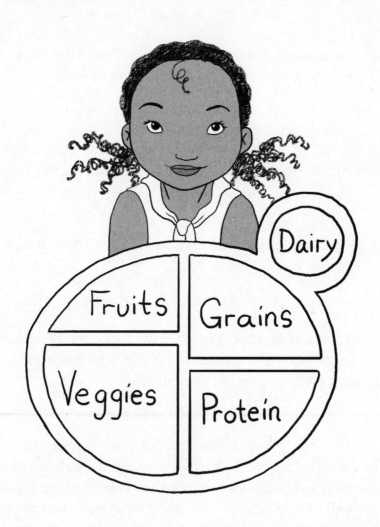

GIRLZ Want to Know

❀ *SUZY: I eat three meals a day like you're supposed to when you play sports and are active like I am, but I get really hungry between meals. I've always heard I'll get fat if I eat between meals.*

Whoever said that was probably a couch potato! If you're like most active girls, three meals are *not* enough to get you through the day. Pack a snack for a midmorning break if you get one at school and one for after school. It isn't even a bad idea to have a glass of low-fat milk before you go to bed. As long as your snacks are healthy foods, like fruit, cheese, yogurt, and peanut butter, you don't have to worry about "getting fat." You're burning a lot of calories in your busy lifestyle.

❀ *ZOOEY: When I can't think of anything else to do, I go to the refrigerator and see what Mom's bought at the grocery store. Is that bad?*

Eating is never "bad" if you're eating because you're hungry. It can hurt you, though, if you're eating just because you're bored or if your habit is to have a bag of chips and a soda every time you turn on the TV or start your homework. Try eating only when you're hungry and then stopping when you're full. When you were little, your parents probably told you to clean your plate, but now you have a better handle on how *you* feel. As long as you're not going to graze on junk food later, there's no need to lick the platter, especially if your stomach is telling you there's no more room.

❀ *KRESHA: Should I be taking vitamins too?*

Most doctors agree that if you're eating a good diet (ChooseMyPlate.gov can help!), you don't really need vitamin supplements unless you have a proven deficiency in one of them. But knowing what the various vitamins do to make you healthier and more beautiful might encourage you to eat those good-for-you foods.

- **Vitamin A** gives you bright eyes and smooth skin. You'll find it in yellow fruits, veggies, and spinach.
- **The B Vitamins** provide energy. They're found in meat, fish, poultry, leafy greens, dried beans, and whole wheat foods.
- **Vitamin C** helps prevent colds and makes strong teeth and bones and great muscles and gums. Oranges, strawberries, broccoli, and spinach are good sources of vitamin C.
- **Vitamin D** makes strong teeth and bones, so drink milk and eat eggs, salmon, and liver.
- **Vitamin E** gives you soft skin, bright eyes, and a healthy liver and lungs. Eating green veggies, nuts, avocados, and sunflower seeds will give you the vitamin E you need.
- **Calcium** builds bones and helps your posture. Dairy products and broccoli (yes, broccoli!) contain calcium. Girls your age need three to four glasses of milk a day.
- **Vitamin K** promotes healing and is found in broccoli, spinach, lettuce, and cheese.
- **Iron** makes good blood, so be sure you're eating red meat, baked potatoes, raisins, and whole grain bread.

Your Food 'Tude

Since we have to eat to live, what we eat is pretty important. We do need to think about it. But, on the other hand, we don't have to obsess! What you think about food is as important as what you eat, and when we're talking about attitude (the way you think and feel about something), you always need to go to God to make sure you're on the right track for you. Here are some things you might discuss with God in your next quiet time:

- being unhappy with the way your body looks
- eating too much
- not eating enough
- eating too much junk food
- not having a balanced diet at home
- not *liking* healthy food
- feeling like a geek because you care about nutrition and none of your friends even give it a thought
- feeling so overwhelmed that you don't have *time* to think about food in addition to everything else

God wants you to be healthy, but He doesn't want this whole nutrition thing to be a drag. After all, He wants your mind clear for listening to Him. So pray for His help in whatever way you need it. Ask for a healthy food 'tude in Jesus' name, and it shall be given. If you still have food issues, let Mom help, and be sure to read chapter 8.

Just Do It

I promised you that the food thing could be fun, so let's prove it. Below you'll find spaces for a day's worth of menus. Look at the MyPlate illustration on page 72 and ChooseMyPlate.gov to review what's in the various food groups. Fill your menu with food you like. Then see if you can arrange to eat the meals you plan soon. You'll be surprised how yummy eating healthy can be.

❀ *Breakfast*

Grain group _____

Bread group _____

Fruit group _____

Milk group _____

❀ *Midmorning Snack*

Grain group _____

Fruit group _____

❀ *Lunch*

Grain group _____

Grain group _____

Veggie group _____

Dairy group _____

Protein group _____

❀ *Afternoon Snack*

Grain group _____

Fruit group _____

Veggie group _____

❀ *Dinner*

Grain group_____

Grain group_____

Veggie group_____

Veggie group_____

Dairy group_____

Protein group_____

Now go back and add a little bit of fat to each meal (butter on your bread or salad dressing on your salad) and one sweet treat for the whole day. Enjoy!

Lily Pad

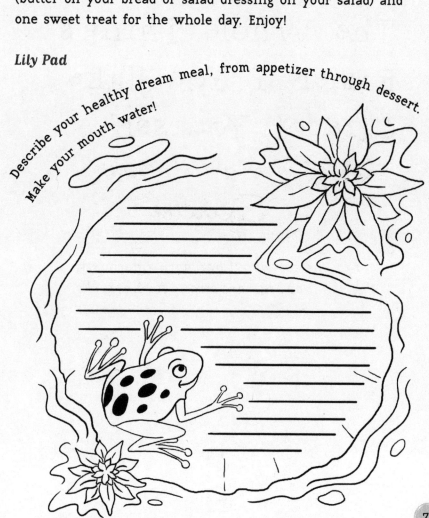

Describe your healthy dream meal, from appetizer through dessert. Make your mouth water!

Seven

The Whole Thing's Easier If You Take Care of Yourself:

Exercise

She sets about her work vigorously;
her arms are strong for her tasks.

PROVERBS 31:17

Attention, All Couch Potatoes!

Yeah, I know some of you are thinking, *Leave me alone! I hate playing sports. I'd rather curl up with a book. Besides, I'm not fat!*

Relax, ladies! Here's some good news for you:

- You don't have to play sports to get exercise.
- You can still spend plenty of time with that book.

And here's some *important* news for you: exercising isn't just about losing weight. It's about

- having energy to do the stuff you like to do
- sleeping better
- making your muscles stronger and more flexible (you'll look better if they are!)
- strengthening your heart and, yes, even at your young age you need to do that
- burning fat
- building your confidence
- taking care of that temple because, yes, exercise *is* a God thing

Okay, Okay, So I Need to Exercise—But How Much?

Under each question, circle the letter by the answer that sounds the most like you. Then we'll talk about what, if anything, you need to do to get yourself on the right exercise track.

1. *I do aerobic exercise (exercise that raises your heart rate and speeds up your breathing)*
   A. every day for at least two hours.
   B. about three times a week for at least twenty minutes.
   C. as little as possible!

2. *When I exercise, either by choice or by force(!), I breathe*
   A. so hard I can't talk while I'm exercising.
   B. hard enough that I can't sing, but I can talk fairly easily.
   C. just like normal because I don't exert myself unless I absolutely have to.

3. *When I'm exercising, I'm thinking about*
   A. how I'm doing, whether my heart rate is right, and how long I'm exercising.
   B. how much fun I'm having.
   C. when it's going to be over.

4. *In my daily activities, I*
   A. keep moving all the time, hardly ever sitting down for very long.
   B. move around a lot, but I also enjoy being still once in a while.
   C. move around as little as possible.

5. *If I have to go somewhere a few blocks from my house, I*
   A. ride my bike at top speed or run.
   B. walk.
   C. get somebody to drive me.

6. If I went on a two-mile hike today, I would
   A. probably beat everyone to the finish point and barely be breathing hard.
   B. probably be breathing harder than usual, but I'd have fun.
   C. be half-dead after the first mile.

Now take a look at the letters you circled. Figure out which letter you chose most often. Then look to see how that adds up.

If you circled mostly A's, you're definitely getting plenty of exercise—which is great. But pay attention to how your body feels while you're exercising or playing. If, while you're exercising, some part of your body hurts or you feel nauseated or your head starts to spin, stop right away and sit down. Those symptoms mean you're overdoing it. Listen to your thoughts too. Are you really enjoying being so active that you almost never sit down and relax? If so, go for it, girl! If you can't honestly say you're enjoying the pace of your life, look at your many activities and see which one or two you might let go of in order to give yourself time to catch your breath. There is such a thing as *too much* exercise.

If you circled mostly B's, your fitness plan seems right on target. You're getting enough exercise, and—maybe even more important—you're enjoying it. If you like what you're doing to keep your body fit, you're more likely to keep doing it—and doing it for life!

If you circled mostly C's, darlin', you need to get out of the recliner more often and get your body moving even if you are currently Stick Woman. Maybe you aren't the athletic type, but that doesn't matter. You can walk the dog, ride your bike, climb trees, and get your friends together regularly to dance. As long as you spend at least twenty minutes three times a week doing something aerobic (your breathing and your heart rate speed up), you're benefiting from it. You may not be able to keep it up for twenty minutes at first, so go for ten or even five and build from there. I guarantee you'll feel better and have more energy for the things you like to do.

The Right Stuff in Exercise
GIRLZ Want to Know

❀ *LILY: I see a lot of older people, like in their thirties, doing all this stretching before they run. Are they just showing off, or is it because they're old that they have to do that?*

Actually, stretching doesn't have anything to do with either age or impressing someone. All of us, whatever our age, should (1) warm up before we exercise and (2) stretch after we exercise. If you're running, start slow rather than taking off like a bullet. If you're going to play a sport, do a few easy laps or some light exercises to start. That will get you mentally ready and will warm your muscles to prevent injuries. Muscle pulls and tears can put you out of commission for a while, and, uh, they hurt! Stretching is important when you're finished. As your heart rate and breathing are slowing down, do some gentle stretches. It will prevent cramping and keep you from being stiff and sore the next day. You won't be walking around like an old lady!

❀ *RENI: I was watching an old exercise video, and everybody on it was bouncing as they stretched. Are you supposed to do that?*
No! In fact, let's go over some guidelines for stretching.

- **Stretch really slowly.** Being the first one back to the locker room is not worth an injury, is it?
- **Don't bounce.** Bouncing was a popular move back in the eighties, but since then we've discovered that bouncing up and down can actually hurt your muscles if they're not stretched out.
- **Hold the stretch.** Once you're into a stretch, breathe deeply and count to ten. If that's too long at first, hold the stretch as long as you can and work your way up to a ten count over a period of days.

❀ *SUZY: My gymnastics coach makes us wear all these knee pads and things when we're learning a new move, but isn't that just because he'll get in trouble if any of us gets hurt? I don't have to do that when I'm working on my own, do I?*
You should. It's always better to be safe than sorry. When you're riding your bike, wear a helmet. When you're playing basketball, wear high tops. When you're practicing your sport on your own, wear the same protective gear your coach

insists on at official practices and games. No one's trying to turn you into a wimp, but why get hurt if you can prevent it?

KRESHA: *I love to roller-skate at the rink, but every time I go, my mom makes me take a water bottle because she says I sweat so much. I feel like a geek hauling that around!*

Your mom's right. Your body keeps you cool by producing sweat, but you need to be taking in those fluids by drinking water before, during, and after your exercise session. There are all kinds of fun water bottles. Find one you really like and drink it till it's empty when you exercise. (It's okay to refill it and drink till it's empty again!)

ZOOEY: *I know I'm supposed to get exercise, but I'm such a klutz. I'm just so uncoordinated! I always mess up the games, I can never hit the ball or do whatever I'm supposed to be doing, and everybody either laughs at me or yells at me because I'm making the team lose. I hate it!*

Maybe you'll always be the one who cheers the team on from the sidelines, and that's okay. But you won't always be as uncoordinated as you feel you are right now. Your whole body is growing, but not all the parts are growing at the same time. That means your arms and legs won't always do exactly what you want them to. You may even feel like you're all elbows and knees! This stage will pass, but until it does, know that exercise will help you become more in control of your body.

But you probably don't want to do your coordination training out there where everyone can tease you, huh? I don't blame you! So start out doing something you can do by yourself, like walking or using an exercise DVD at home. Or ask someone you trust not to poke fun at you to teach you how to play badminton or swim the backstroke. Although some people *are* more naturally athletic than others, everyone has to learn by doing. The more you do something, the better at it you'll be. Who knows? You might be out there playing volleyball with the team after all!

Just Do It

Let's play around with this whole fitness thing. On the one-week calendar that follows, fill in the physical activities you're already doing—soccer practices, dance classes, the five-minute walk home from school.

If you see that you're already exercising three times a week for twenty minutes at a time, pat yourself on the back and keep it up. If you're *not* exercising three times a week for twenty minutes at a time, plan that kind of exercise and put it on your calendar. And don't forget to . . .

- do fun things, like dancing, no-brainer, no-skill games, and hiking to your favorite spot.
- do practical things, like walking to school, raking the yard, and riding your bike to your friends' houses.
- get someone to hold you accountable for keeping to your exercise plan.
- reward yourself when you've had a good workout. Munch a few peanut M&M's, read your favorite book for the umpteenth time, or take a nap in the hammock.
- exercise three times again next week!

Talking to God About It

As always, tell God everything you're thinking and feeling about fitness and exercise. He'll listen to every word, no matter how lame it may sound coming out of your mouth! Tell Him everything. If you need some help getting started, try this approach:

Dear _____ (your favorite way to address God),

I really do want to take care of this temple, my body, because I know it's sacred to You. I wouldn't let the church building get all cobwebby and dusty if it were my responsibility to clean it, so I guess I can't let this temple go either. But I need Your help.

*My biggest problem with exercising is _____
_____.*

When it comes to exercising or playing sports, I hate being teased about _____.

When I think about sports and fitness and all that, I worry about _____.

While we're on the subject of fitness, God, I'm sorry that I _____.

Will You help me with _____
_____?

Thank You for making my body _____
_____.

I love You!

Lily Pad

If I could be a star in any physical activity—anything at all—it would be _____. In fact, I can imagine it right now, in detail . . .

Eight

Don't Trash Your Temple

You are not your own [but God's]. . . .
Therefore honor God with your body.

1 CORINTHIANS 6:19-20

You're at a point in your life when your parents aren't around you all the time anymore, and you're being influenced by many more people, by teachers, school administrators, friends, older kids at your school, counselors, pastors, and the list goes on. That expanding world is normal and healthy, and it helps make you a strong, well-rounded person.

But it can also present you with challenges, situations you'll have to make decisions about, and choices that will make a difference in how you treat your body. You may have already made a vow to yourself never to let any of these things touch your body:

- cigarettes, cigars, tobacco of any kind
- alcohol
- illegal drugs, including marijuana

You may even have gone so far as to decide you're always going to have good sleeping and eating habits. Maybe you're committed to protecting every part of yourself from harm. If you have, good for you!

But do keep in mind that even the strongest vow can become wobbly if

- everybody else is doing what you've vowed not to do
- everybody else seems to be having *fun* doing it
- everybody else seems so grown-up doing it
- you figure that it's *your* body and nobody else's and that you can realistically do whatever you want to it
- you realize your body is the only thing you *do* have control over right now, since everybody else controls your behavior and your time and where you live

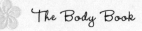

You get the idea, don't you? It's downright hard out there in the world to keep the promises you've made to yourself *if* you don't rely on God to help you keep those promises.

How Is This a *God Thing*?

We already know your body doesn't belong to just you: it belongs to you *and* God. Let's look at more passages like the quote at the beginning of this chapter:

> *Don't you know that you yourselves are God's*
> *temple and that God's Spirit lives in you? If anyone*
> *destroys God's temple, God will destroy him; for*
> *God's temple is sacred, and you are that temple.*
>
> 1 CORINTHIANS 3:16—17

What we need to focus on now is how much we need God in order to remember this truth. The bottom line is we can't stay away from tobacco, alcohol, and drugs without God's help! If you're going to say no to drugs when everybody who's anybody is doing them and enjoying them, you have to remember this:

> *God is faithful; he will not let you be tempted*
> *beyond what you can bear. But when you*
> *are tempted, he will also provide a way out*
> *so that you can stand up under it.*
>
> 1 CORINTHIANS 10:13

If you're going to say no to alcohol even when all the cool people are drinking it, you *must* keep this promise in mind:

> *Submit yourselves, then, to God. Resist the*
> *devil, and he will flee from you.*
> JAMES 4:7

If you're going to say no to that cigarette when you're really curious about what it's like to smoke one, you *gotta* remember what Jesus said:

> *"Apart from me you can do nothing."*
> JOHN 15:5

If you're going to go to sleep at a decent hour when that cute boy wants to talk on the phone half the night, or if you're going to eat a healthy amount of food even though all the models in the magazines look like they starve themselves, or even if you're facing what seem like lesser temptations, please, please, please keep this in mind:

> *It is God who works in you to will and to*
> *act according to his good purpose.*
> PHILIPPIANS 2:13

Make time to strengthen your relationship with God *every day*, and He'll be there for you when your promises to yourself are put to the test. He'll help you say no in a way that may even help somebody else say no too.

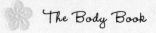

"Evils" We Don't Think About Much

You've probably been hearing about the evils of drugs, alcohol, and tobacco since you were in second or third grade! But there are some other temptations adults may not have discussed with you. Let's take a peek at a few.

❀ *Could You Turn That Thing Down?*

What teen or tween *doesn't* like to listen to her music loud and clear? But be careful! Loud music, especially coming through headphones, can damage your hearing over time. Once you lose your hearing, you won't get it back. So next time you put your headphones on and crank up your music, have somebody stand beside you. If she can hear the music coming out of your phones, turn it down until she can't. You'll thank me later!

❀ *Night Owl!*

Your body's rhythms (called *circadian rhythms*) may change at puberty. You might, for instance, find yourself wanting to stay up late at night and sleep in—*way* in!—in the morning. Unfortunately, most school schedules and other responsibilities don't work around that, so you need to establish a good sleep schedule and help yourself get to sleep on time. You need to get shut-eye for school, even if all your friends are yakking on their cell phones until the wee hours, or even if you'd rather stay up with a flashlight and read that great book.

Who Am I?

Are you getting enough sleep and the right kind of sleep at the right time? Circle the answer to each question that best describes you.

1. I wake up in the morning

   3 pretty energetic and ready to go after a couple of minutes.

   2 sleepy, but I can function pretty well within a half hour.

   1 ready to blacken the eye of the person who woke me up. I don't really wake all the way up until about noon.

2. Every night I get

   3 at least eight hours of sleep and sometimes more.

   2 eight hours of sleep but sometimes a little less.

   1 a lot less than eight hours of sleep.

3. The amount of sleep I get

   3 is almost the same every night, no matter what day of the week or what time of year it is.

   2 is the same every night during the week when I have school, but it varies on the weekends and during vacations.

   1 is different just about every night.

4. I go to sleep

   3 almost as soon as my head hits the pillow or at least within fifteen minutes.

   2 pretty soon after I go to bed, although sometimes I lie awake for maybe a half hour or an hour.

   1 hours after I go to bed—or am supposed to go to bed. Sometimes it seems like I lie awake half the night.

5. When I sleep

   3 an atomic bomb could drop, and I wouldn't wake up.

   2 I don't wake up until morning unless there's a lot of commotion.

1 I wake up a lot, sometimes with nightmares or because I'm worried or something scares me.

Now add up the value of the numbers you circled: _____

Before we go on, let me remind you that no score is bad. Some scores just mean you may want to pay attention to certain things. You want to be sure you're getting all the rest you need to be happy, healthy, and beautiful!

If your score is between 13 and 15, you're a pretty efficient sleeper, and you seem to be on a good schedule. Keep up those good habits of sticking to a regular bedtime and getting at least eight hours of sleep (if not more!) every night. You're doing a lot to keep your body healthy.

If your score is between 9 and 12, you have some good sleep habits, but if you want to be at your very best, look at your 2 and 1 answers. Which of those areas do you want to fine-tune first? For help with how, read the bulleted list of hints that follows.

If your score is between 5 and 8, you're dealing with sleep deprivation and being cheated out of feeling your best. It's probably not exactly your fault. After all, we can't just flip a switch and automatically sleep until the next morning! So here are some ways you can help yourself get the rest you need:

- Go to bed and get up at the same time every day, no matter what day of the week or what time of year it is. Once you start sleeping better, you can give yourself an occasional sleep-in treat.
- Get a bedtime routine going that you follow every night: do the same get-ready-for-bed things in the same order. Maybe you'll take a hot bath, crawl into bed with your journal, turn on some music, and take fifteen or twenty minutes to unwind. Some girls like to listen to nature sounds. Others like to read a couple of paragraphs before they doze off. Try not to make your ritual sacking out in front of the TV.
- Exercise regularly, but don't do it within an hour or two of bedtime.
- Don't drink or eat anything with caffeine after about 8:00 p.m. That means soda, coffee, tea, and chocolate.
- Don't eat a big meal within an hour or two of bedtime either. If your tummy's growling at bedtime, just drink a glass of milk.
- If you're worried or excited about something before you go to bed, talk it out with someone or write about it in your journal before you hit the sack.
- Never go to bed all wound up. Do some gentle stretching, take a hot bath, or rock in a rocker. There's nothing worse than getting into bed and flopping like a flounder because you can't settle down!

- If you can't sleep night after night or if you're plagued by nightmares every night, talk to your mom and dad. Your parents, a doctor, or a counselor can help you, so don't let not sleeping well go on without telling someone. Life is too much fun for you to be too tired to enjoy it.

By the way, if bed-wetting is a sleep problem for you, you're not alone. *Enuresis*, as it's called, happens to a lot of girls (and guys). It's because your bladder is too small to hold all the urine your body makes during the night. Don't despair! You'll grow out of it. Meanwhile, your doctor can give you one of several different kinds of medicines to keep it from being a problem. There's hope for those sleepovers yet!

Food Nightmares

You've probably heard of eating disorders like anorexia and bulimia. Even if you know something about them, they're so dangerous it's worth reviewing them one more time.

❀ *Eating Disorders in General*

When a girl becomes so obsessed with losing weight that she stops eating normally, chances are she has an eating disorder. In fact, no matter how thin she is, when she looks in a mirror, she sees a fat girl. So she may go from eating less and less to throwing up what she does eat, taking too many laxatives, swallowing diet pills, and/or exercising until she drops. Unless she gets help, she'll get physically sick. She could damage her body permanently or even die. Eating disorders are that serious.

❀ Anorexia

A girl who has anorexia nervosa will basically try to starve herself. She thinks about avoiding food all the time. When she does eat, she uses certain rituals to keep from eating what she considers too much. She'll do things like cut her food up into small pieces so it looks like she's eaten, eat very slowly, not touch her mouth with the fork, or play with her food. As she gets thinner and thinner, she will start having physical problems and may have to be hospitalized.

Usually it takes intense counseling of some kind to get a girl with anorexia back to healthy eating.

❀ Bulimia

A girl with bulimia also wants to be thin, but she tries to accomplish this by eating a whole *bunch* of food in a short period of time (that's called bingeing) and then forcing herself to throw it all up—and she does this day after day after day. She too will become physically ill if she doesn't get help. Initially she'll suffer from stomachaches, sore throats, and even tooth decay, but the ailments can get much more serious.

✿ When to Get Help

A lot of the things we've talked about in this book have been just normal parts of growing into a young woman. Other things aren't, like:

- sincere hatred of your own body
- menstrual cramps that put you in bed or keep you from doing your normal activities
- periods that last longer than eight days or occur fewer than twenty-one days apart
- being severely overweight
- an addiction to drugs, alcohol, or cigarettes
- extreme insomnia (not being able to sleep)
- anorexia
- bulimia

If you're experiencing any of these things, you *really* need to talk to your parents about getting some help. There's no shame in going to a doctor or a counselor. In fact, being willing to reach out for help shows real maturity. Know that God does *not* want you to be miserable, and He sure doesn't want you to suffer alone. As always, pour out your problems to Him. Every challenge has a solution. Always.

Just Do It

We've been talking about some heavy stuff in this chapter. Let's lighten up and look at your blessings, okay? Taking a look at how very good your life is can help you steer clear of the pitfalls.

- One thing I love about my family is _____
  _____.

- One thing I love about my best friend is _____
  _____.

- My favorite part of the day is when _____
  _____.

- I'd rather eat _____ than anything else.

- I love to go to _____.

- I love to wear _____.

- I feel loved when _____.

- I can't wait to _____.

- The thing I love best about God is _____.

- I know God loves me because _____.

Doesn't that feel great? You have a lot going for you, girl. Don't waste an ounce of energy on things that aren't good for you.

Lily Pad

If I had a friend who had a problem that was hurting her, I would . . .

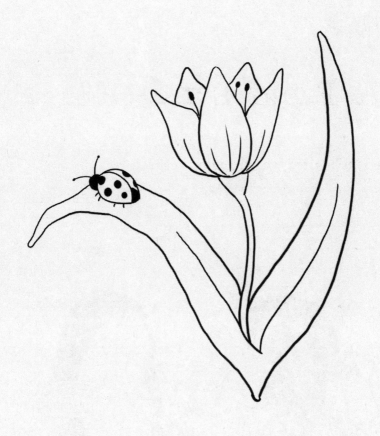

Nine

A Final Send-Off

A kindhearted woman gains respect.

PROVERBS 11:16

Remember God-Confidence?

If you've read *The Beauty Book*, you may remember us talking about the kind of confidence that makes you beautiful. It's the same kind of confidence that makes you glowing and healthy, that makes you want to take care of and respect your unique body. Let's review.

Have you ever known a girl who wasn't exactly in sync with the rest of the girls when it came to her physical development? Maybe she didn't have a sign of a breast or she had enough breasts for three people. Yet the more you got to know her, the cooler she seemed because not only did she respect everyone and treat them more than decently, but she treated herself the same way.

You look good when you *are* good. You look beautiful and you feel beautiful when you are sure of yourself. A lot of people call that *self-confidence*. It's really *God-confidence*.

Who Am I?

See for yourself. Stand in front of a mirror. Smile at that girl looking back at you as if you like her and accept her and want to be her best friend. Now watch what happens when you look at her as if you hate her guts. Which girl looks better, no matter what her breasts or her skin or her waistline is doing?

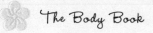

How Is This a *God Thing*?

You can have that God-confidence that makes you beautiful and mature because

- God carefully chose each of your features and combined them to make *you*.
- God's idea of inner beauty is a lot more important than the outer standards that airbrushed models offer.
- Jesus talked only about inner beauty, and if you've got Him, you've got that, baby!

Now might be a good time to stop reading and just say, "Thank You!" to Him.

It's a Lifelong Thing

We've also been talking about all this body care and upkeep as if it were a puberty thing. But the stuff we've covered is stuff you'll need to pay attention to your whole life:

- understanding what's happening inside your body at any given time—like when you get married, when you're pregnant, after you've had a baby, and when you're starting menopause (which is kind of like the reverse of puberty!)
- paying attention to what your body is telling you (are you hungry? thirsty? tired?)
- liking and respecting your body
- nurturing yourself when your period gives you a bad time
- wearing comfortable bras
- eating a nutritious diet

- getting the right amount of exercise
- avoiding cigarettes, illegal drugs, and the abuse of alcohol
- getting the right amount of sleep
- not obsessing about weight so much that you hurt yourself
- getting the help you need if your struggles become more than you can handle
- always having a woman in your life you trust and can talk to
- going to God with everything and knowing He's there for you

If that way of living becomes second nature to you now, you're going to have a much happier, healthier, and problem-free life than if you don't develop these good habits. This is *forever* we're talking about, and forever starts right now!

The Bennies

Just in case you aren't yet con-vinced that your body is worth all this attention, let's list the benefits in plain, prac-tical language:

- bright eyes that see the world as only you can
- sharp ears that can hear all the world's best sounds, including the voices of the people you love
- a sound, alert mind that can stay focused on God and

learn how to live the glorious life He has planned
for you

- a clear voice that can tell the truth about God's love
to the world
- the strength and energy to do all that God asks you
to do (you'll never have to offer some lame excuse!)
- a heart that beats with kindness, respect, and God-
confidence
- a body that's ready to do all that God calls you to do as
a woman and to be the best you can be as you do so

A Private Word

Just a final word before I leave you, and that's about privacy.
As you become more and more aware of your body, reserve
the right to keep it private, even from your own family.
This list may help you see what I mean.

- It's perfectly normal for you to want to keep your
bedroom door closed when you're changing clothes or
when you just want to be alone. If you share a room,
it's still normal to want some private space somewhere.
- You shouldn't have to endure people coming into the
bathroom when you're in the tub or on the toilet if
you don't want them there.
- It isn't a sign that something's wrong with you if
you feel shy or self-conscious changing clothes
or showering even in front of your best friends.
Some people are more modest than others. You are
respecting yourself when you set boundaries around
what makes you uncomfortable.
- If you have to see a doctor for any reason—especially a
gynecologist, who specializes in women stuff—you have

the right to ask someone to explain to you exactly what's going to happen and even to request a female doctor if that would make you more comfortable.

- If a person touches you in a way that makes you feel uncomfortable, no matter who it is, *immediately* tell an adult you trust. Don't try to protect someone who is hurting you. Your body is yours and God's. Keep it as protected and as private as you want to.

Who Am I?

All right, girl, let's take one last quiz to see where you are now that you've read all about puberty and had a lot of your questions answered. You may even want to come back and take this little checkup once every couple of months. You'll be surprised by how much you change, how much you grow, and how close you'll get to being a *woman!*

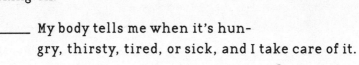

Which of the following statements reflect the way you think? Put a check mark by those. Don't check any you don't yet do or truly believe. The blanks will show you what to keep working on.

_____ My body tells me when it's hungry, thirsty, tired, or sick, and I take care of it.

_____ When it comes to keeping clean, I'm there! I shower or bathe every day.

_____ Exercise is something I do a lot. It makes me feel great.

_____ When people talk about drugs, alcohol, and smoking being bad for your body, I agree because I know that stuff'll hurt me.

_____ If somebody touched me in a way I didn't want to be touched, I'd immediately tell an adult I trust.

_____ I don't compare myself to other girls. I know we all develop according to our own unique schedules.

_____ If I could change one thing about my body, I wouldn't do it.

_____ I eat a pretty healthy diet most of the time, even when I'm not at home.

_____ I'm okay with the whole period thing.

_____ I get plenty of sleep.

_____ I have my moods, but they don't control me.

_____ I'm a girl and I love it!

_____ I know God has a plan for me, and I'm keeping myself in the best shape possible so I can carry it out.

_____ I go to God all the time for help with all of the above!

Lily Pad

If I had a little sister who wanted to know what it was like being an almost-woman like me, I'd tell her . . .

Check out this excerpt from the fiction
companion to

The Body Book!

The Lily Series

Lily Robbins, MD

Dairy

Fruits | Grains

Veggies

Protein

by Nancy Rue

One

Psst! Snobbins!"

Lily Robbins didn't have to look up from the pizza boxes she was carrying to know that voice. It was Shad Shifferdecker, the most obnoxious kid in the entire sixth grade. She tossed her mane of red hair and, as usual, ignored him.

And, as usual, he persisted. That was one of the things that made him so obnoxious.

"Snobbins!" he hissed again. "Are you gonna eat all that pizza yourself? Dude!"

Lily just kept moving toward the door of Little Caesars. *Just a couple more steps and I'll be away from the absurd little creep*, she told herself. *And the sooner, the better.*

She leaned against the glass door and pushed herself out into the January-freezing air.

"See ya tomorrow," Shad said behind her. "If you can get through the classroom door—" The Little Caesars door slapped shut, and Lily hurried toward the maroon van where her mom was waiting with the motor running and the heater blasting. Even though Lily couldn't hear him anymore, she knew Shad wasn't finished with her. He never was.

Don't look back, she warned herself. *Or you'll see something gross.*

Still, just as she reached the van, she caught a glimpse

of her mom's face. It was twisted up into a question mark as she stared inside Little Caesars. Lily couldn't help it. She glanced over her shoulder—and immediately wished she hadn't.

There was Shad, at the door, his whole jacket crammed inside his T-shirt and his cheeks puffed out to three times their normal size so that he looked like a demented version of the Pillsbury Doughboy.

You are so *not funny!* Lily wanted to shout at him. Instead she flipped her head around and stomped toward the van.

Or at least she *tried* to. On her second step, her heel slid on the ice, and she careened crazily forward, juggling pizza boxes and heading for a collision with the frozen ground.

The pizzas hit first, with Lily landing right on top of them. Through the box she could feel the warmth of the grease against her cheek. The smell of pepperoni went right up her nose.

Above her she could hear the van window on the passenger side going down.

"You all right, Lil?" Mom said.

"Yeah," Lily answered through her teeth.

"Is the pizza all right?"

Lily moaned and peeled herself off the pile of slightly flattened boxes. "I bet all the toppings are stuck to the cardboard now," she said.

"Don't worry about it," Mom said. "Just get in the van before you freeze your buns off—and our dinner gets cold."

Lily did, although she wasn't as worried about her buns *or* the pizza as she was about the story Shad Shifferdecker was going to spread to their whole class tomorrow. But she didn't even risk a glance inside Little

Caesars as she climbed into the van and examined the top pizza.

"I think it's okay," she said while Mom was backing out of the parking place and mercifully leaving Shad behind. "Just some pepperoni stuck to the lid, but I can peel that off."

"And I would if I were you," Mom said dryly, "before your brothers get a look at it and want to know what happened."

"Mom, please don't—"

"How much is it worth to you for me to keep my mouth shut?"

Mom's mouth was twitching the way it always did when she was teasing. She would try hard not to smile, but the twinkle in her big, brown doe-eyes always gave her away.

"You're not gonna tell," Lily said.

"Who was that delightful child in the pizza place?" Mom said, lips still twitching. "Friend of yours?"

"No, he is *not*! Gross!"

"Come on, now, Lil. Don't hold back. Tell me how you really feel."

"I can't stand Shad Shifferdecker," Lily said, inspecting pizza number two. "He can*not* leave me alone. He's in my face all the time, telling me my hair looks like it's on fire or my mouth looks like Angelina Jolie's or my skin's so white it blinds him when I'm out in the sun."

"Charming," Mom said. "And how's the pizza? Art will go ballistic if his sausage is mixed up with his Canadian bacon."

Lily pried open the lid to the pizza on the bottom and wrinkled her nose. "How do you know whether it's messed up or not?" she said. "It always looks like somebody already ate it to me, with all that stuff on there—"

"Lily! Hold on!"

Mom's arm flew out toward Lily and flattened against her chest. Swerving sharply, it suddenly felt as if the van were out of control. Lily looked up just in time to see a pair of taillights in front of them disappear as their van spun around. Headlights glared in their faces.

"Mom!" Lily screamed.

She squeezed her eyes shut and, for some reason she could never figure out, clutched the pizza boxes against her. She felt the van lurch to a stop, and she waited for the crash that was surely going to kill them both. But all she heard was her mother's gasp.

"Oh, dear Lord!"

Lily opened her eyes again. The other car had spun once more and was sailing across the road, straight toward a pickup truck coming from the other direction. As Lily and her mother watched, the two vehicles slammed together and crumpled like . . . like two pizza boxes.

Metal smashed. Glass broke. And then it was as quiet as snow itself.

"Dear Lord," Mom said again. Only this time her voice was quiet and grim as she reached for the cell phone and punched in three numbers.

"Do you think anybody got hurt?" Lily said.

She knew the answer was obvious, but it was the only thing that came into her head.

"There's been an accident on Route 130," Mom was saying into the phone.

How could somebody not *get hurt in that?* Lily thought. She shuddered and tried not to think of what the people inside must look like.

Mom hung up the phone and grabbed her winter gloves. "I'm going to go see if I can do anything before the paramedics get here."

"You're going *over* there?" Lily said.

"I'd want somebody to come help us if we'd been the

ones who got hit." Mom pulled her knit cap down over her ponytail. "And we almost were."

A chill went through Lily, and it wasn't from the blast of frosty air that came in as her mother opened the van door. *It could have been us—all crumpled up and maybe bleeding—*

It wasn't a thought she wanted to be left alone with. She got out of the van and followed her mother, picking her way across the ice.

"Lil, why don't you stay here until I know what's happened," Mom said.

"I want to come," Lily said. Her own voice sounded thin and scared.

"Then get some blankets out of the back. And the first aid kit."

Lily didn't even know there *was* a first aid kit in the van. It didn't strike her as a Mom kind of thing. Whenever Lily or her younger brother, Joe, or her older brother, Art, got hurt, Mom would say, "Are you hemorrhaging? Have a bone sticking out?" When the answer was no, she'd tell them to go get a Band-Aid and not whine about it. But there *was* a first aid kit in the back of the van, along with two blankets and even a pillow. Lily grabbed all of it and made her way over to the side of the road.

Mom was there with some other people who had stopped to help, and they were all crouched around somebody on the ground. As soon as Lily got close, Mom put her hand up and said, "That's far enough, Lil. Just leave the stuff here."

There was no merry twitching around her mother's mouth now. Her tan face was white, and her voice was strained. Lily backed away, her heart pounding.

"Could we have one of those blankets over here?" someone said. Lily looked up. There was a teenage boy, around Art's age, crouched down beside a small person. The child was sitting up, so it was probably safe to go over there. Lily grabbed one of the blankets she'd just set down and slipped and slid across the ice to get to them. "I don't think he's hurt," the teenager said to Lily, "but he's shaking like he's freezing."

Lily squatted beside him. A boy of about five blinked up at Lily, his face the color of Cream of Wheat. His lips were blue, and the teenager was right: he was trembling like a leaf about to fall off a tree.

"You want a blanket?" Lily said to him.

He didn't answer, but Lily wrapped it around him anyway and then rubbed her hands up and down his arms, the way her dad did to her when she was whining about being in danger of frostbite if she had to walk to school.

"I don't think he's hurt," the teenager said again. "He's probably not, huh?"

Lily looked up at him in surprise. He was shaking as badly as the little boy was, and even in the dark Lily could see tears shimmering in his eyes.

"He doesn't look like he is," Lily said.

"Nah, I bet he's not."

The teen crossed his arms over his chest and stuck his hands into his armpits. His bottom lip was vibrating.

"Did you ask him?" Lily said.

"He won't say nothin'! He just sits there—but he's probably not hurt."

The teenager just kept shaking his head. Lily got the strange feeling that the kid didn't really know what he was saying. Mouth suddenly dry, Lily turned to the little boy.

"What's your name?" she said.

The little blue lips came open. "Thomas," he said in a voice she could hardly hear.

"I'm Lily," she said.

"Lily," he said.

The teenager let out a shrill laugh. "You see! He's not hurt, huh?"

"Do you have any *owies*, Thomas?" Lily said.

"What's an 'owie'?" the teenage boy said.

But before Lily had a chance to say, "You know, a boo-boo, a cut, or a scrape, or something," the air was filled with the screaming of sirens. The teenager's face drained, and his eyes went wild.

"I just lost control!" he said. "It was the ice! I couldn't help it!"

His voice was so full of fear that even little Thomas started to cry. Lily put her hands on his arms to rub them again, but he stuck his own arms out and hurled himself against her. There was nothing to do but fold him up in a hug.

"It's okay, Thomas," Lily said to him. "You're okay."

The teenage boy was *not* okay. The minute a police officer got out of his car and started toward him, he broke into tears. It made Lily feel like she wanted to be somewhere else. Fortunately, the policeman took him aside. But then little Thomas started to whimper.

"You're okay," Lily said. "You aren't hurt. It's okay—"

"I am too hurt," Thomas said.

Lily pulled him away from her a little and looked at him. "Where?" she said.

"My tummy," he said. "It hurts a lot."

"Oh," Lily said.

She looked around for someone to call to, but the flock of uniformed adults who had just arrived all seemed to be either running around or hovering around the person on the ground. Lily looked back at Thomas. He was bending over at his waist now, and his eyes were looking funny, like he couldn't quite focus them.

"Um . . . why don't you lie down? I'll get somebody to help us," Lily said.

"Don't leave!" Thomas said, and he clutched at her sleeve with his fingers. Lily noticed for the first time that he didn't have gloves on, and his little fingers were red and stiff.

"Okay, but lie down. And put these on."

She peeled off her knit mittens and slid them over his tiny hands.

Then she got him to curl up in the blanket with his head in her lap.

"You smell like pizza," he murmured.

It was the voice of a person who was about to fall asleep, and it scared Lily. She twisted around and caught sight of a paramedic walking away from the person on the ground, right toward them.

"This one okay?" the paramedic called to her.

"I don't think so," Lily called back. "He says his stomach hurts. And his eyes look funny and his lips are blue and he's falling asleep."

The paramedic's steps got faster, and he already had his little flashlight out when he got to them.

"Hey, fella," he said to Thomas as he shined the light in his eyes.

"His name's Thomas," Lily said.

"Stretcher over here!" the paramedic called out. "We're gonna have to take you to the hospital, Thomas," he said.

"Mommy!" Thomas said.

"Mommy's going too, only she's getting a different ride. You'll see her when you get there."

"You come with me."

Thomas was looking right at Lily, his eyes trying hard to stay focused.

"Is this your sister?" the paramedic said.

"I didn't even know him before tonight," Lily said.

The paramedic grinned. "He sure likes you." He went on doing things to Thomas as he talked. "Thanks for staying here with him. The other driver told us he thought he was all right." He grunted softly. "'Course, he has a reason to want him to be all right."

Thomas whimpered, and Lily leaned down over him. "You *will* be all right, Thomas," she said.

"Sure he will. All right, fella. We're gonna put you on this stretcher and give you a wild ride. How would you like that?"

Thomas's face puckered weakly. "I want *her* to take me."

"Tell you what," said the paramedic as two other people in navy blue down jackets lifted Thomas like he was a feather and put him on a stretcher. "She can walk with us to the ambulance. How would that be?"

Thomas nodded, and Lily scrambled to her feet and got as close to the stretcher as she could without getting in the way of the IV bottle that was already suspended above him. She knew what that was; she'd had one herself last fall. It was much better being on this side of the stretcher. She could put her hand out to Thomas and hold his as she hurried along to the ambulance, and she could talk to him and reassure him that everything really was going to be okay.

He still wailed for her when they slid him inside the ambulance, and she would have jumped right in there with him if any of them had given her half a chance. But they closed the doors behind him, and the first paramedic put his hand on Lily's shoulder just before he headed for the driver's seat.

"Thanks for your help," he said. Then he jumped into the front of the ambulance and started the siren as they pulled out of the icy slush and back onto Route 130. As Lily watched them go, she could almost hear the paramedic adding, "And, Lily, you're welcome on our team anytime."

Check out this excerpt from the first nonfiction book in The Lily Series!

The Beauty Book

The Lily Series

The Beauty Book

by Nancy Rue

You Gotta Love It

LORD, you are our Father.
We are the clay, you are the potter;
we are all the work of your hand.

ISAIAH 64:8

You Gotta Love It

Okay, let's get one fact straight right up front: every girl has her own special beauty.

Yeah, I know you've heard your mom say, "Well, *I* think you're beautiful, honey." I also know that doesn't mean a whole bunch when some kid's calling you Pizza Face or everybody's telling your sister she's drop-dead gorgeous and then patting you on the head and saying, "You're cute too, honey."

But really, God doesn't make junk. He made each of us just exactly the way He intends us to be. So just like everything else God made—from blackberries to rhinoceroses—*you gotta love it*. You gotta love *you* too.

"Yeah," you may ask, *"but if every girl is beautiful, how come "everybody" isn't seeing it that way?"*

Because—bummer!—people aren't like God. Somewhere along the way, since the whole Adam and Eve thing, somebody decided there was only one way to be a beautiful woman at any given time. Right now that standard is being five foot ten, weighing about a hundred pounds, and having lips as big as the living room couch.

So how are you supposed to convince "everybody" that you're this knockout even though God shaped you like a fire hydrant or gave you lips the width of a pencil line or gave you curves nobody else has at ten?

You can't. You only need to convince *you*, and that's what this book is about. By the time you get to the end, I want you to be able to check yourself out when you pass a store window and say, "That's me. Cool! And I love that!"

Here's a good way to start. From now until you finish reading this book, try to follow this rule: NO BAD-MOUTHING THE WAY YOU LOOK.

That means no dwelling on the zits that have appeared on your forehead. No talking about how fat you think you are. No wishing you had curlier hair (or smaller ears or straighter teeth). Pretend you are one of your friends. You would rather eat brussels sprouts than hurt a friend's feelings, right? So NO putting your friend—*you!*—down.

That's a really hard rule to follow, so let's look at some of the things that can keep you from seeing how gorgeous you are.

BEAUTY BLOCKER #1: TV TRAINING

One of the reasons people think there's only one way to be beautiful is because that's all they see on television and in magazines and movies and on the Internet. Even the Barbie dolls seem to scream, "You have to look like me!" But you don't.

GIRLZ Want to Know

❀ *LILY: Those girls on the cover of* Seventeen *have perfect skin. How do they get that?*

They don't. Nobody's skin is that perfect. Everybody has at least the occasional zit, freckle, or scar from when she crashed her bike. Those magazine photos are retouched with computer programs and digital editing software that can remove "blemishes" (why don't they just call them pimples?),

make eyelashes longer, and even chisel in great cheekbones. If you met those models in person, you would see that they have pimples, birthmarks, and little scars too. No lie.

❀ *ZOOEY: If I use the shampoos and face creams I see in the ads, will I look the way the models do?*

Probably not. For starters, that model isn't you. And don't you think if a company wants to sell a product that's supposed to give you thick, shiny hair, they're going to pick a model who *already has* that thick, shiny hair? Besides, if you were born with thin hair, there isn't much in this world that's going to make it thick. But who says you have to have thick hair to be beautiful?

❀ *RENI: I'm the shrimpiest girl in my whole class. Why does God even make short girls when tall girls are always the ones people think are beautiful?*

Actually, people's ideas of what's beautiful change over time. Back in the late 1500s and early 1600s, plump women with rolls of rosy flesh were considered beautiful, mostly because the better fed you were, the wealthier that meant you were. In the 1950s, lots of curves were the going thing in the movies and on the posters. By today's standards, Marilyn Monroe would have been considered overweight, but men in the fifties drooled over full-figured women. In the 1960s, when the Beatles said on the radio that they preferred petite girls, everybody wanted to be a short little peanut.

Does that mean somebody who *was* beautiful forty, fifty, or four hundred years ago *wouldn't* be beautiful today? How much sense does *that* make? Nah, *this* makes sense: everyone has beauty—plump and rosy, round and curvy, short and pixie-like, *and* tall and pencil slim, not to mention everything in between.

BEAUTY BLOCKER #2: THE COMPARISON GAME

Come on. We've all played it.

"I don't have breasts yet, so I'm not as grown-up as Chelsea, but at least I don't have to wear those geeky braces like Whitney, so I can't be *that* bad."

It seems like a harmless enough game. After all, most of the time you just play it in your mind until you come out ahead of somebody and can make yourself feel better, right? Well . . . hmm. Let's see what God has to say about that.

How Is This a *God Thing*?

It used to be the "thing" to wear bracelets and T-shirts that said *WWJD: What Would Jesus Do?* You could even get it on boxer shorts, for Pete's sake! The trend has passed, but the question is still worth asking: What *would* Jesus do when faced with the temptation to make Himself feel like He was okay by playing the comparison game? Would He say to Himself, "Yikes! I don't have big muscles like Peter, so I must be pretty wimpy. Then again, Peter's always asking stupid questions. I must be smarter than he is. That's more important, right, Dad?"

Of *course* Jesus would never say that because Jesus was perfect. We will never be perfect, but we do try to be more like Him, right? And if the above is too lame for Jesus, it's too lame for us too. Dad, uh, *God* certainly doesn't compare us. Can you imagine God saying, "I sure did a great job on Carly's complexion. Too bad I messed up on Emily's. She's not nearly as cute." *Hello!*

God doesn't compare us. Jesus doesn't compare us. The world we live in compares us, but who are we supposed to follow?

Jesus made it really plain. Love your neighbor as yourself (check out Mark 12:31). That means no putting your "neighbor" down—and no putting yourself down. Period.